P9-DDC-838

MULTITUDES

Publication of this book was supported by grants from the Eric Mathieu King Fund
of The Academy of American Poets and the National Endowment for the Arts.

Also by Afaa Michael Weaver

Water Song (1985)
My Father's Geography (1992)
Stations in a Dream (1993)
Timber and Prayer (1995)
Talisman (1998)

MULTITUDES
POEMS SELECTED & NEW

AFAA MICHAEL WEAVER

Sarabande Books
LOUISVILLE, KENTUCKY

Copyright © 2000 by Afaa Michael Weaver

FIRST EDITION

All rights reserved

No part of this book may be reproduced without written permission
of the publisher. Please direct inquiries to:

Managing Editor
Sarabande Books, Inc.
2234 Dundee Road, Suite 200
Louisville, KY 40205

LIBRARY OF CONGRESS CATALOGING-IN-PUBLICATION DATA

Weaver, Afaa M. (Afaa Michael), 1951–
    Multitudes : poems selected and new / by Afaa Michael Weaver.
        p. Cm.
    ISBN 1-889330-40-X (cloth: alk. Paper) — ISBN 1-889330-41-8
    (pbk.: alk. Paper)
        I. Title

PS3573.E1794 M85 2000
811'.54 21—dc21   99-046428
                                                           CIP

Cover image: *Black Face and Arm Unit (1971)*, by Ben Jones. Used by
permission of the artist.

Cover and text design by Charles Casey Martin.

Manufactured in the United States of America.
This book is printed on acid-free paper.

Sarabande Books is a nonprofit literary organization.

for
Marva J. Weaver
Sankofa

ACKNOWLEDGMENTS

The author would like to thank the editors of the following publications where some of these poems first appeared, sometimes in different versions:

African-American Review: "The Poets," "African Jump Ball," and "Enemies"

Unsettling America: "The Black and White Galaxie"

Artist and Influence: "Kings"

One Trick Pony: "Lamentations #1-3"

American Poetry Review: "Radio Days"

Women's Studies Quarterly: "Eighteen"

Long Shot: "Mojo Mamba" and "Composition for White Critics..."

Furious Flower Anthology: "The Poets"

"Ego," "Beginnings," "An Improbable Mecca," "Back from the Arms of Big Mama," "The Madman Raises the Dead," "Meditation for My Son," "New England," "Luxembourg Garden," "My Father's Geography," and "Homecoming" are from *My Father's Geography*, by Michael S. Weaver, © 1992. Reprinted by permission of the University of Pittsburgh Press.

"A Maxim," "The Final Trains of August," "Mass Transit," "Going to the Church with C.W.," "My Son Flies to Visit Me in Providence," "Tuna Fish," "Sub Shop Girl," and "Bootleg Whiskey for Twenty-five Cents" are from *Timber and Prayer*, by Michael S. Weaver, © 1995. Reprinted by permission of the University of Pittsburgh Press.

"The Poet Reclining," "Self-Portrait," "The Tree of Life," "The Birthday," "Lovers with Flowers," "Solitude," "Adam and Eve," "Bathsheba," "David," and "The Praying Jew" are from *Stations in a Dream*, by Michael S. Weaver, © 1993. Reprinted by permission of Dolphin-Moon Press.

"Borders," "Water Song," "A Young Aristocracy," "A Photograph of Negro Mania," "To the Vietnam Vet," "South African Communion," and "A Life in a Steel Mill" are reprinted from *Water Song*, by Michael S. Weaver, © 1985. Reprinted by permission.

"The Robe," "Michele," "Humility," "Writing Numbers," "Mt. Zion Baptist," "Mama's Hoodlum," "Sin, 1969," "The Incomplete Heart," "Friendship, 1994," and "House Training" are from *Talisman*, by Michael S. Weaver, © 1998. Reprinted by permission of Tia Chucha Press.

CONTENTS

❖

Timber and Prayer

Talisman

New Poems

INTRODUCTION

We watch for contented artists
who sign bloodless treaties with despair...
Afaa Michael Weaver, "New England"

A faa Michael Weaver is not a contented artist, although we might forgive him for being satisfied with his remarkable accomplishments as a poet. If Weaver has signed any sort of treaty with despair, as surely he must have done in order to survive as a black American and grow as an artist, it is not a bloodless agreement, but a passionate *entente*. The poems in this volume, shrewdly chosen from five previous books and including some new pieces, amount to a compelling presentation of the mind and art of an important writer. Weaver's vision is rooted in an African-American culture that he specifically knows, not astray in some overly mythic representation. His vision is local and focused, and as befits a poet of genuine depth and seriousness of purpose, it is as wide as the horizon itself.

Clearly learned in and influenced by Anglo-American as well as African-American writers, he is yet an original, with a moving body of work distinctly his own. In the hard-won tradition of African-American poets dating back at least to Phyllis Wheatley in the late eighteenth century (Weaver pays homage to her here), he emerges now as a brilliant part of that tradition. Weaver also finds a place in the legacy of Whitman and the mid-nineteenth century when in the evolution of American poetry the glory of vernacular speech first became fused in verse with an inspired sense of the American self, sensuous and yet transcendent. Weaver's verse acknowledges the guidance of that tradition and honors it.

As a craftsman, Weaver commands our respect. The range of his poetical language stretches wide. It takes in, on the one hand, an almost homespun simplicity that sacrifices nothing in the way of

xiii

intellectual urgency, emotional weight, or imagistic brilliance. On the other extreme, and certainly in some of his latest poems, such as "The Last Jazz Club" and the climactic "Composition for White Critics," we see the collagist and surreal daring as painfully appropriate to the creativity of a writer for whom madness is a major theme, impelled both by private loss and the chronic insult of social injustice. At its most typical, Weaver's line flows as easily as the common, unaffected speech he clearly prizes; this clarity reflects the balance and harmony, the sanity and benevolence, to which his entire poetic and personal questing aspires.

Diligently exploring the expressive potential of his community (which includes both black and white America), and doing so with a startling variety and facility, Weaver has made himself into a virtuoso in his manipulations of vernacular form. His skilled adventures into blues and rap narratives, though relatively few in his body of poems, are inspired. His efforts in these forms are not simply imitative or parodic of street culture but amount to an almost uncanny absorption of blues and rap into the bloodstream of his art even as he preserves a more literate and meditative central identity as a writer. He fuses the tragic, the erotic, and the richly comic, and he does so with a brilliance beyond the scope of virtually all the many other published poets who, like Weaver, pay homage to the blues tradition as a guiding presence in their lives and art. Poems such as "Mojo Mamba" and "Piggly Wiggly"— Rabelaisian send-ups of black American phallocentric humor, where the folkloric boastings of "Shine" and John Henry slip easily into postmodernist rap—are composed so deftly that one is brought up short when the exaggeration and the laughter stop and the meditative voice and rhythms return to serve the poet's more intimate needs.

Weaver's depiction of black culture clearly emerges from a profound love of black people. Yet he is painfully aware of the variations, some of them toxic, within that culture. His work explores the tensions of class that arise between a poet who defines himself as an artist and the masses of people for whom poetry is both a luxury and an unabashed feature of their daily lives. In his masterful "The Poets," for example, about a basketball game between two high schools, one virtually all-black, one virtually all-white but attended by the poet, Weaver explores the harrowing divide that can exist between the poet and the people who are both "his" people and outside his circle of intimacy, perhaps forever. One of the few, integrating, "privileged" blacks at the virtually all-white school ("we sang pep songs in German, peeping / inside our shirts and ties at our own / magic"), the poet is stirred by the non-chalant genius of his school's black rivals: "The Dunbar poets [the team's official nickname] made baskets / while strolling, dreaming of rivers"). This poem touches on some old questions never far away in Weaver's self interrogation—questions about the phenomenon of psychological and cultural double consciousness, so brilliantly defined by W.E.B. Du Bois, and the fate of the African-American *savant*.

> *I am 18 years old, and I write poems*
> *on the backs of tally sheets for the tin.*
> *I read Du Bois and James Weldon Johnson.*
> *The white men hate me. The black men*
> *don't trust me....*

Another strong impression here is of a poet confident about the subjects of his art; Weaver knows what he must write about, and he is not easily distracted by fashion or politics. While he is alert to the lessons of African-American history, to issues of gender, race, and class, his obsession as a writer is centered in the self and not in ideology. There is no question as to which is more important. The self is shaped both by circumstance—by nationality, "race," gender, chance (as in the death of his first son, which may be the central sorrow of his life and his art)—and by forces more elusive. We see Weaver's world through the eyes of an intensely private and personal self, which both embraces the public sphere and holds it at bay.

The dearest and most potent social commitment for Weaver is to family, tightly identified here by the poet's father and mother (about whom many of these poems are written, including the most heartfelt), his sister and brother, aunts and grandmother, his own and other children. His family is the community writ small; the community is his family writ large. These are "ordinary" African-American lives, forged by the down-South legacy of slavery and Jim Crow brutality, the enormous but optimistic disruption of the Great Migration north, and the playing out of the dream of freedom and progress in the cities of the North, especially in Baltimore, the city of the poet's youth. Their lives are a balance of idealism and material ambition, endured as much for their children as for themselves; and the home is proof of progress and a bulwark against the forces that would keep them down. The reward of the poet's elders came hard:

> *Every day on time and some sixteen-hour shifts*
> *paid for the cars, the suits, the promises,*
> *the grand feeling of buying a new row home.*
> *It was the best the world would give then*
> *to its best workers, blacks, browns, high-yellows*
> *from the South. It took us children thirty years*
> *to believe it. Now we are grateful.*

At one level, slavery and the historic black American past are hardly more than flickering shadows in these poems; at another remove, they form a constant presence. This is so, in part, because the idea of black victimhood is as repugnant to the poet as it was to the black men and women who brought him up. While the poet is fascinated by history, and explores it directly here and there, he is more concerned with filtering the past through the lens of the present, revealing the subtle effects of history on individual lives. There is much feeling here, of pleasure and pain, but virtually no sentimentality, grotesquerie, or impulse to blame others. What matters most is the nurture of family and the sometimes painful lessons passed on from one generation to another, not always successfully, about life, and especially about life as a black American.

Unlike the work of some gifted black poets drawn to themes such as the African slave trade, the dreaded Middle Passage, and the horrors of American slavery, Weaver shows little interest in history as panoramic spectacle or epic narrative. Still less is the past a kind of ornate museum. History lives most effectively in the present, in the continuum of the black experience. Black history is epitomized on a modern, domestic scale, in a domestic place, notably in the now ghostly house of his youth, through the poet's depictions of individuals who live their lives in the modern moment but with a constant haunting by the ordeal of African-American history.

While the beauty and dignity of black American culture are profound concerns here, Weaver brings a strong sense of compassion to his depiction of the outer, or white, world. He searches for wisdom and understanding whether he is describing a beloved older acquaintance or a neurotic young man thoroughly despoiled by racial hatred. The poet has earned his right to be so benevolent. He has seen and known the other faces of deceit and racism, and recognized them for what they are. In his determination to make sense of America as a culture, to impose order on its chaos, to assert the fact of its beauty over the parallel fact of its capacity for moral squalor, the poet ignores neither its reality or his own integrity.

Unifying the world for this poet is his generally unstructured but potent faith in the power of God, which places all hurt and harm in an annealing perspective. Not only the promise of grace, but also the narratives and the languages—the poetry—of Judeo-Christianity, draw him to this fountainhead as they have drawn countless other literary artists. So too does the never to be forgotten experience of religion as encountered in the African-American churches of his youth, or as lived broadly by his father, who "believes in the Resurrection and good bourbon."

The theology, ritual, and social purposes of the black church blend powerfully to instill in the young poet an instinct for seeing the world in moral and religious terms. Yet in an unjust world, God can often loom as a sinister presence. "I have felt God tinker with man's differences," Weaver writes about venturing into the racist South, "moving through our quartered spaces, / making strangers of the same flesh and blood."

Nevertheless, Weaver's profoundly-humane dedication to life leads him to a different sense of what divinity can bring to our existence despite all our troubles and divisions. God then is no specter, but a supreme force for good:

Inside I listen for him to enter me,
to flow into this infinite cavern of my heart
and help me know this quiet village
behind me and the solitary angel above,
as other sanctities beg in my shadow,
offering foreign altars and hymns.

—Arnold Rampersad
Stanford University

*The individual is part of the conscious human race
or he is an animal grubbing for sustenance.*
                                              —Julius K. Nyerere

*Myself. I'll act more wisely toward the world:
I'll place my eyes right at my fingertips
and only see what my two hands can feel.*
                                  —Sor Juana Inés de la Cruz

Water Song
1985

Borders

I have seen lines on a paper
turn four-lane highways to roads
snaking through clusters of pine,
raise foot-high grass in medians,
pull the tongues of people to a drawl,
tighten the air and fill it with honey,
put the hands of women on their hips,
stand them in peanut fields with straw hats,
slow the paces of men to a crawl and sit
them on the gas pumps of one-room stores,
scratch belligerence in the eyes of whites.
I have gone South in summer nights,
watching the sun rise haughty and oppressive.
I have felt God tinker with man's differences,
moving through our quartered spaces,
making strangers of the same flesh and blood.

Water Song

In the house that has died,
the dead come down wooden stairs at noon,
puffing the cotton curtain, a cramped bunch
of light pressing down step by step burning,
stopping at the dining room, sitting on
plastic table covers, circling the window,
then they jet through the empty mansion
chasing each other, embracing the empty space
where Granddaddy's picture was kept until
the fall from grace, the deaths in the water,
the water of the lake all around the house,
holding the life still there at siege,
jealous mirrors bobbing on small waves
that swallow and fill the lungs with screaming.

No man knows his time, but his time is appointed.

The slipshod mules with box heads and flies,
collar and reins worn to brown frazzle and fiber,
darkened and hardened corn scattered in feed bins,
an empty smokehouse with padlock opened and rusted,
covered outhouse dumps sinking, the old house
flapping its open door back and forth admitting,
garden patch aside going broke under weeds and snakes,
the back porch where we bathed and pinched the girls,
a Victorian mansion of wood and tin and screens,
its skin thinning, its bones going hollow and ashen,
its mind blossoming out and over the farm, growing.
Down the path behind the corncrib there is still
the crack of bushes beneath his feet, fallen pine
branches snapping under the crush of his hands,
the restless moan of the mules bemoaning his call,

his call away, the intonation of angels in his ears,
coming down to turn the home into an ugly wailing,
there is still the flailing of arms in lake water,
armies of people in the abandoned home, discarnate.

The dead come back to old folk in the country to talk.

An empty swirl of leaves, empty but for the ghosts,
has fallen in through the window, swirling on the floor,
bronze, yellow-gold, black, crisp as paper,
popping up and down on gray, painted floors,
the lives take hold and breathe in the decay,
travelling down the hallway where Grandma slept,
gushed by sudden air into the living room where
summer visitors from up north slept and whispered,
back into the kitchen against the hard iron legs
of the stove, they dance and shout echoes,
a shudder in the house and they are gone back,
following evening rays back to the sun, sucking
back to the moon at night, instant glitter
on the roof, then nothing but dull tin and
the evening gossip of angels when the lake
slaps a wet tongue on muddy banks and steep falls.

In the twinkling of an eye, in the twinkling of an eye.

Homemade brooms of straw, bundles wrapped in twine,
skirting the wooden floor, scraping the rough finish,
hands dipped into white, metal washbasins, cupped
in prayer, rubbing against faces grimy with oil,
headless chickens tied to upturned poles, flapping
their wings in anger, feathers filling the yard,
hogs grunting over slop, sleeping in their food,
a pair of hands operating the udder of the cow,
raw milk spraying against the bucket in squirts,
bowl upon bowl of hot vegetables toted to the table,

potbellied stove churning an inferno of wood,
in the house that has died and is decaying,
there is laughter, prayer, singing, cursing,
the blare of radios, inordinate snoring from a farmer
who sang his own eulogy as he walked to the lake,
sirens like Egyptian handmaidens over the deepest
move of waves, Canaan in the splashing of catfish,
in the house that has died and is decaying, a shell
of a place where people no longer live in flesh.

Death holds no fear for folk who are Christians.

Grandma sits on the back porch in a metal glider,
riding silently back and forth, cobwebs in the corner,
her spittoon from a Campbell's soup can
by her foot, through the door comes a sucking
energy like a giant, empty heart with open arms.
She goes again back into the mist of it
with all of them, all the blood of the farm
that has gone to the water and all the plethora
of death, all the endless ways of leaving
in the air over the farm, among the million
blades of grass pushing up, in the clearings
between the pines, a harsh crackle from CB radios,
an ambulance starting up from the lake weighed
by a sudden journey to Canaan, through and past
the lake. The life slips free over the fields.

I will be back in the by and by. Dying ain't forever.

In the house that has died,
the dead come down wooden stairs at midnight,
soft feet like cotton shuffling to the front porch,
sitting down to dangle over the edge, examining
the picnic table where children ate watermelon.
Granddaddy sits in his corner, napping, sleeping

in the nest of a big, empty heart, a sucking energy,
a song like Egyptian handmaidens over the lake,
the dark, moving silence around this world.

A Young Aristocracy

On their weekends off from the mills,
my father and uncles drove their new cars
to Turner's Station, the mill smokestacks
in the distance, their lungs still feeling
the scratch of the soot they took for air—
in three- and two-piece suits with big shoes,
their Virginia and Carolina ways in a big city.
My mother and her sisters sat on the porches,
in white dresses with ankle socks and patent
leather like dark images of the Andrews Sisters.
Every day on time and some sixteen-hour shifts
paid for the cars, the suits, the promises,
the grand feeling of buying a new row home.
It was the best the world would give then
to its best workers, blacks, browns, high-yellows
from the South. It took us children thirty years
to believe it. Now we are grateful.

A Photograph of Negro Mania

Sitting on cracked and peeling marble steps,
riding in worn-out limousines hanging over the chassis,
struggling up city street hills waddling with
sweating backs, exposed to overeating and ads and ads and ads,
fist-sized hearts imprisoned, sentenced to beating
through uncharted miles of untoned and suicidal flesh
     whispering, "Lord."
Whispering "Lord" over and over, turning fish in pans,
beating the rising dough, filling pie shells, feeding
starving masses flashing through alleys past richochets
of bullets, standing on swollen ankles, radios crackling
    with morning spirituals.
Stages with mohair suits and precision dancing,
artistic genius with classic starvation setting jazz
to geometric progression, sages in African zoot suits
with saxophones, the lead given to bass players when the leader
falls in a pool of sweat, vibraphones beat with blinding
flurries of minute and hairy tongs, the songs, the greatest
    burp of childlike people.
On trains with cardboard suitcases filled
with fried chicken, potato salads making greasy eyes
on the sides, peeping Southern eyes on the passengers, the North
whipping past the windows in a blur of trees, coming in 1902,
1943, 1960 and before there was ever a clock or civil rights
worker to count them, coming in pre-Columbian trinkets
to lie in Cuba in shallow graves and the bottomless hells
    of the Smithsonian and cultural indignance.
Thirty million of them whooping and dancing on the head of a pin,
under the eye of Jesus, their preachers the epitome of Saturday
night conmanship, their mahogany elegance a tune in four-four,
the haphazard zazen of classical Bach and heathen jungle drums
    suddenly becoming percussion.

Unashamed, unashamed, unfree and brought up right,
respecting the smooth glow of moonshine and stars,
the striking stink of rubbing alcohol cooling their grandmother's
heels in her winters, the Beatitudes and poison ivy in vacations
                    in the hell of the South.
Sitting quietly, still as pre-storm summer air,
taking Kool-Aid popsicles, frozen custard, melted Hershey's,
turning fried eggs in grease of old bacon, frying cornbread,
bending our skin-shiny heads saying evening politely to the age
                    and darkening white shadows.
Up the one-lane highways through the Carolinas and Virginia,
bouncing on shifting droplids of Chevrolet pickups,
turning paper fans for four hours on Sundays, eyes peeled back
at the boredom, occasional possessions doing foot stomps
in the aisle, the Holy Ghost descending on a church where bootleggers
sell in the woods, where wet mouths chew gum and love notes,
                    up through gates to heaven's where.
In another spring, renewed, full of insight, humbled,
blackness is something revered falling on unwilling hearts
like the veil of night—this misery, these smiles unsummoned
in the alleys, rusted Cadillacs, fish frys, church dinners,
dark bars, shooting dice and drinking wine, dying, falling out,
                    making a grand appeal to life.

To the Vietnam Vet

It must have been like a funhouse,
walking the high cliffs under rock apes,
dodging the large stones they tossed down,
lifting the black death to shoo them,
when the women were as cheap as cigarettes,
dutiful, lasting as long as the dollars.
In the jungle night must have felt like
the plumage of a giant peacock around you,
a billion eyes still as pursed lips on
your arms. I remember this when I approach
your house on foot, peeking under cedar
bushes for feet other than the slanting trunk,
taking cover under the first lamplight.
When you peek from your window smeared with
paint, I know it is you and not the black
patriot sleeping in shit with dead men,
remembering Martha & The Vandellas,
afraid to call out to soldiers who
declared it was not your war. Strange
thing when they fire vets from jobs because
they remember, because they stand still
for a moment like sailors tied to a mast,
weathering the storm of phantoms. Stranger
still that I must write a hundred songs
for your unpainted army because I want
you all to believe I understand.

South African Communion

It is not difficult to feel compassion
for the workers in South Africa that stand
in half-mile lines waiting to board buses,
down the dirt roads of shanty towns to mines
and auto factories, the hats with headlights
passing ore up to the bosses, tight-lipped
and fervently religious with their usurpation
of God. At night in South Baltimore we take
excursions from company property to the bars
downstreet, the convenience stores in the heart
of white condolences. The faces we meet, the blank
smiles, the beckoning fists, the yells are
grandchildren of laws that did not allow blacks
to set dusty foot on white pavement past nightfall,
did not allow excursions, the woolly growths to be
called afros, or brown fingers grasping books—
nothing pretentious and black but the night itself.
It is not difficult to understand greed here
where freedom has been harvested, cut and laid aside
to die, when a whole other paradise was carved
from theft. The whole arrangement comes clear.
It's the times I look down and see the dark brown,
veiny hands beneath white frowns, or the scowering
shadows of neon lights from 7-11's and police
sirens, when a waitress would rather not touch my hands
with the change, when a cop calls me *boy* when I'm thirty,
when people force laughter over clenched knives. It's just
a joke and not very difficult to feel compassion
for the workers in South Africa standing mute in predawn,
hustling to houses of relatives and friends at night
with passes underlined with photos, tossing stones
at personnel carriers. It's easy travelling the streets

of Baltimore, searching the shadows for psychotic cops,
clutching the passport licenses to drive and be seen,
against the impregnable shadows of the moon over
the hatred.

A Life in a Steel Mill

My father is proud of his life making pipes,
his small row home, his five children, his peace,
two week vacations he took in summertime,
hauling us in his '54 Ford to Lawrenceville,
his wife throwing her arm around him.
He likes to think he was able to pay for good times,
crab feasts in public parks, Saturday drinks
with my uncles while his wife cooked hot soup.
He is as steady as a mountain at rest,
in movement he has the force of an inland river.
He believes in the Resurrection and good bourbon.
He is grateful for the life work has afforded.
My father is a burning sun, an oracle of flesh,
the damp crush of morning dew on naked feet,
a crack and screech of wooden wagons in tobacco,
a host of empty echoes like thunder in caverns
of steel mills, the clatter of his buddies
at a roadside bar coming in town from work.
My father is a son of the ten thousand things.
My father is hickory, tears I have never seen
come through buds in springtime to become leaves.
My mother in her death is the wind and rain.

My Father's Geography
1992

Ego

God's voice
is caught in
the crackling commotion
of thought,
like dried leaves—
breaking.

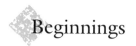

Beginnings

for Gene F. Thomas

The house on Bentalou Street
had a cemetery behind it,
where the white hands of ghosts
rose like mist when God
tapped it with his silver cane.

There were giant cedar trees
out front that snapped when
we hit them from the porch,
jumping like big squirrels
from the stone ledge.

Inside it had no end;
the stairs led to God's tongue;
the basement was the warm door
to the labyrinth of the Earth.
We lived on the rising chest of a star.

And on one still day,
I hammered a boy until
he bled and ran, the blood
like red licorice on my small hand.
The world became many houses,

all of them under siege.

An Improbable Mecca

for Ted & Emma Sharp

I am here in the house
of my childhood, my youth,
of the quiet and whisperings
from walls that have watched
me lose my two front teeth
to a cousin slinging a baby doll,
walls that have recorded
the saltatory eruptions
in the living room floor
where the whole of us learned
the premeditated Manhattan
and the snap and flare
of the *Bossa Nova*, the Twist,
here in this house where quiet
ruled like an avenging saint
even when I rolled, drunk and dirty,
in the living room at seventeen,
home from college with hoodlum friends,
in the year of the Black Quartet.
This house opens its eyes,
reaches to me with hands held
together in silent prayer,
begging me to take every lesson
and go on with life peacefully,
out of its contemplation,
out of the lives it has absorbed,
out of my father's pondering step,
coming home in the evenings
in his brown leather bomber jacket,
ecclesiastical and provident,
out of my mother's discordant
singing as she put yellow ribbons

in my invalid grandmother's hair,
singing old spirituals being quickly
removed from new hymn books,
always falling back to her favorite,
"Pass Me Not, O Gentle Savior."
Her humble cry resounds
in the tiny mind of my ear
when I slide my hands down the walls
as I ease down the stairs of
this house where Mother and Grandmother
died, where the bones of this home
screamed until they were thin
as glass when I lost my mind.
This house throws back its head
and laughs in a resplendent roar
that goes up in bubbling clusters
when I ask it to remember
the first poem I wrote at eight,
the Sears & Roebuck bicycle
with whitewalls and headlights,
the first girlfriend in the fourth grade,
the first wife at nineteen,
the long hours of studying,
the lectures on ancestry from Grandma,
the delicate cloth of talking
and sharing I built with my father
as we became the next two
on the prophetic end of the pew,
the anxious, sleepless nights
while we listened to Bessie
frying the chicken for the trip
down home, south to Virginia,
back to the embracing roots
that made us believe unfalteringly
that we were truly wealthy,
the pious Sunday mornings

when I marched off
to the Baptist church quiet and measured
like the Methodists and Lutherans,
with my usher's badge and my belief.
This house stands before me
and in my memory, a monument
perfectly aligned to the stars,
luminescent and sentient,
a life in and of itself and ourselves,
as patient and kind and suffering
as anyone could ever hope a house
to be when chattering children
kick in its lap, men lie in it,
trying to accomodate their future,
when women paint it with song
from the old world of patriarchal law,
when death comes lusting after it
with sledgehammers and stillness—
I come to the front steps
and sit as I did when I was a child
and hope that I can hold to this
through life's celebrations and calamities,
until I go shooting back
into the darkness of my origin
in some invisible speck
in an indeterminable brick
of this house, this remembering.

Back from the Arms of Big Mama

—an avuncular song for Alya Amani McNeill

In this room, in this chamber,
the sun stands like a woman
in an old cotton dress in August
shelling peas under maple shade.
In this room your great-grandmother,
Big Mama, slept away under the eyes
of the council of her daughters,
who kept a vigil, a deathwatch,
rocking back and forth in their chairs,
humming unexpected hymns,
huddling close together, making room
for the angels, seven feet tall
in blue pin-stripe suits with silver
lights for eyes. Your great aunts waited
in this room where my mother
watched the door in the firmament
as these angels walked away with Big Mama.
Here my mother agreed to die.
And here I hold your entire body,
one month into the world,
brought here by my baby sister.
I show an old rough face
that has laughed and cried
with lips that want to pucker
against your candy cheeks.
I feel like a giant
suddenly discovering in his hands
the delicate and splendiferous
fragrance of the first breaths
ever taken by a tiny life,
my hands that have struck,

22

my hands that have caressed,
my hands that have pulled
against the hem of heaven.
I want to give all,
all that I own and may earn
so that you might have peace,
give all like St. Francis of Assisi
to lessen the pain and tears,
to make you go into the cavern
of this corpulent world
like Sojourner Truth, name
blazing against greed and lies.
I tell you your destiny
for which I am accountable,
tell you how you will grow
and shine brilliant among women,
attend Ivy League universities,
become a doctor when I am old
and desperately in need of one,
how you will not take
any of the shit men give to women,
how you will prosper and know
very little pain as now
the host of thousands
of minute soprano angels
who minister to the newborn
are here chanting a song
for children, something unpretentious
and familiar, like nothing I know.
Each time one of them
leans over to your beautiful ear
and says softly, invisibly,
"Alya, you are home, child,"
you smile and stretch and coo
in the arms of a big old uncle

with a scarred life who has come
through the spirit's wars
still hungry for your wise eyes
stepping forward from the light.

The Madman Raises the Dead

The morticians have a way
of wrapping babies in plastic bags
where gases encase the bodies,
leaving no cuts or loud drainings.
But I washed you myself,
in sweet soap and warm water,
eased your tiny feet in white socks
and finished you with a blue top.

Now in an angel's loud armor,
I kneel near the stone cross above
your grave, watching the grass shudder,

waiting for this night to burn and fall
so that every dead soul that touches
your bones will fill with air and sing.

Meditation for My Son

When I go spinning,
your care is given
to the steel nerves
of reticent angels.

When I cannot hold,
my own heart drops away,
some sure finger from
a faded portrait follows
you in the thorn-filled
curves of man's road.

When I cannot dream,
I pray in blind rooms
that possible colors and bodies
will converge around you,
set you sailing over rocks,
away from the soulless.

When I am not whole,
I entrust you to seraphim
in their difficult dominion.

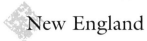# New England

*At night a voice
lends its enchantment,
and New England is owned
by the pondering dead.*

Lovers in the Needles

As twilight set fire
to bobbing hills of snow,
making the tinkling reflections
in the crystals explode
in tiny, brilliant burstings,
she sat alone in the kitchen,
by the shaking window
rattling in the rough groove.
She sat knitting a nightshirt
for the child to come,
sighing for the tiny graves
in the grove of birch and elm,
reciting quietly the prayers
that set their young bodies
in the cold earth and snow.
She sat until she saw
a young sailor running up
the Boston Harbor in April,
mangoes stuffed in his coat,
gulls chasing round the masts
of brigs at the dock, and
he reached for her lips.
She felt flush, then hollow,
her lips pasted on glass;
she opened her eyes,
the snow overcame her again,
her hands fell in the silence

of wood popping and whistling
in the hearth, of shadows
without voice sliding
from wall to vicious wall,
only his militia certificate
and the old, impossible boots
that thrilled and appalled.
Her eyes shot out and around,
the moon had captured her,
full and beckoning,
over the flickering snow.
She put a leaf in the Gospels
and found the rope, marched
slow and weightless, singing
up the stairs, heavenward.
Her benediction came with
the squeaking yell of timber
burdened with her weight,
the swinging dress and collar,
her soft, white feet
pedaling the air above the stool,
her tongue jammed and caught,
as she tried to sing "Amen."

In colonial New England
women braved the winters
and died young. The coffers
were filled with Africans,
molasses, rum, and oil.

The Minister's Compass

Some Sundays when red maples bloom,
I sleep in the Baptist church

squatting in Old Providence's hill,
unbeknownst to the tours,
to old men in herringbone.
I step among them and search
their eyes for the gratitude
their fathers hoped for
as they slept in forecastles.
I look in slavering mouths
for the hallelujahs
to pump up when they think
of who packed the cobblestone,
who delivered the mackerel and cod,
who drifted down Africa's coast,
collecting the naked slaves,
who drummed God in their heads,
who gave the Cross to Indians,
who took this blessed nation
out of heaven's launch
and set her virgin hull
into the world's deep blood.
Stopping, I hear nothing
but cheap chatter of the moment,
and the very next moment,
no vision of the future,
only the indolent stare,
with tidy talk of television.

Moving among the living,
I think of how freedom
is a mandate for everyone,
how I have come to own nothing.
My heart is confused,
a compass on the spin.

Cherubs in the Glen

When the madam paced
the wharves in Boston,
she looked for something special,
a delightful, naked girl
who might have died on board
with greater cargo, but stared
now with pleading eyes,
and she became a Wheatley,
a genius like a warbling finch,
prodigious, gay, and fragile.
She took the breath away
from gaping strangers, turning
the language and fixing it
like someone adorning
a forest with Chinese silk,
pasting the red walls of the Veil
with the human constant.
When they buried
the four fallen from fighting
in the Boston Massacre,
she rushed to her quill
and penned a tribute.
Her heart was full
of song, and when it quit,
she fell dead with a child,
long after the brave lights
held in the Old North Church.
She fell dead with a child,
beyond the plea of Diana,
a woman in colonial New England.
    "To me the meanest flower that blows can give
        Thoughts that do often lie too deep for tears."
Her silver gleanings
were the songs in the elms

above the head of a ship caulker
once a slave who turned
the word again to kindle
the soul's soft string.

The Minister's Heart

From a sermon's midst,
I would catch you in the square,
dark hair flaming deep,
enchanting, a tune rising
from your head like a chorus.
Your soft, counted
movements under the trees
like the slow plucked
strings of a harp halted
my hand holding the quill
until I strode the room,
begging grace not to lift
its lace hem from my head,
begging for the very light
to leave my eyes so I could
take the world through my hands.
That only fed Satan's laughter,
for as I thought of the world,
I thought in an instant
of a frightened flock of finches,
and your hands, the nimble grasp
around the neck of a bottle,
or the assured laugh you gave
to the lies of the fishermen,
as your neck arched white
in the sun, turning a hundred shades
as you walked. I ached

and wept like a green sailor,
pouring my tears on the pages
of the Psalms, banging
Proverbs with a clenched fist.
I stripped to the waist,
beat myself with tight leather
to loosen the domination
of the flesh, but each time
I shamefully touched myself,
it was you my soul cried for,
you my very being denied grace for,
you I wanted to wrap
in the black leaves of my coat
and press through my naked breast.

Now I have you,
my fingers hold that hair
that derives its power
from the trills of the moon.
At night I pull the cloth back
for the stars to shine
on your filling breasts,
the soft rising of your belly,
to set miniature twinkles
in the toes I paint
with my tongue in the morning.
I hold your head and
am not shaken by the spectre
of Lucifer dancing in the window,
the dance of poor Job,
for I have nothing but my life,
and that I would give
for you. In the mornings
when you bring the blueberries,
I hold your hand as long
as prudence will allow in the day,

before the serpent's head
rises in the pious eyes,
before God's rage goes shouting
in the woods, beating wildly
from tree to anchored tree,
and I am held to you
by the flame of breast on breast,
the sense of immortality
I feel when I gaze
on the crown of your thighs,
a white and auburn bloom
that rules me with its perfume,
that makes my self-flagellation
a mockery of love's florid dignity.

And do not die, never die—
for the Puritan councils
and our entangled exegesis,
I will wear the dread emblem
branded on the flesh of my heart
until it takes my breath,
and I sleep to the Day of Doom.

The Whalers

We were off island
for two weeks, headed
south for the leviathan.
I was on deck sleeping,
the sun burning pleasant
fires in all my pores,
when from the crow's nest,
"Blows. There she blows."
They trampled me,

running to starboard side,
"Get up you old nigger,
there's one of God's beasts
bathing above like
a ship overturned and hull up.
Get your one good hand
you lazy nigger, get it now."
The captain bellowed
to lower the boats,
the whale lounging in the sun,
resting from charting the world,
its great soul giving thanks
in sprays that shot up,
seen for miles around,
talking in thunderous bass
to all the Deep's populace,
issuing kingly demands,
while its death sped on
in cedar whaleboats
with harpoons like razors
and whale lines set
to follow him to the floor.
When they cut him,
he sliced through the surface
as if he had wings,
taking both boats and crew
on a Nantucket sleigh ride,
breaking one, drowning the crew,
taking the other until
it could not budge a fluke,
and the final point
was cast in his eye,
a sin as sure as extinguishing stars,
for I heard him sing
when they did it,
when they cut his lungs

and the thick blood ran,
unsure of a world
it had lived in but never seen.
On board, rolling the blanket piece,
the clouds turned sorrowful faces
in their white juxtaposition,
the scorns of angels
watching a huge saint
undone to the bone,
its dignity boiling in the tryworks,
while I changed the sea water
beneath them with my good hand,
the bad one maimed by a whale
that sounded and took whale lines
and my hand with her,
the hemp burning me to the bone.
This one gave two hundred barrels,
and we plunged farther south,
farther than the Indians dreamed
when they hunted with canoes,
boiling the monarchs of the deep
on beaches in tryworks there.
We headed for the Pacific
and the giant flesh
that swam there in herds
governing the Earth
from Antarctica to the Arctic,
relentlessly hunted by men
afraid of earth oil
and disappearing profits.

And the old whalers on shore
lived comfortably sometimes,
after the storms,
the ships' bones bleaching
like the whales' in the sun.

Provincetown

Ambling through the cape,
we begin at Buzzard's Bay,
stopping in the full moon
to play with an itinerant retriever,
watching his wet body
melt in the trail of moonlight
linking the beach to the gods.
He loses the wood floating
and threatens to drown himself
with determination in the black water,
until we throw more flotsam,
and he yelps to celebrate
the deception, the call away
from the dead end of duty
that swallowed men
and made women suck and choke on
the delicate lace of loneliness.
Driving on, the wail of ocean
is hushed by the towering woods
until we reach the point,
the first landing of Puritans,
where Cook assembled his thespians
in Mary Vorse's old wharf,
looking out the window,
dreaming of some revival,
some Greek organic seed
to deify the American soul,
as O'Neill carved his dark emperor.
We watch for contented artists
who sign bloodless treaties with despair.

At night bright ships sail the sky,
pushed on by the songs of ghosts

given back by history's rituals
for an eternal voyage back to love.

My Father's Geography

I was parading the Côte d'Azur,
hopping the short trains from Nice to Cannes,
following the maze of streets in Monte Carlo
to the hill that overlooks the ville.
A woman fed me paté in the afternoon,
calling from her stall to offer me more.
At breakfast I talked in French with an old man
about what he loved about America—the Kennedys.

On the beaches I walked and watched
topless women sunbathe and swim,
loving both home and being so far from it.

At a phone looking to Africa over the Mediterranean,
I called my father, and, missing me, he said,
"You almost home boy. Go on cross that sea!"

# Homecoming

for Kala Weaver

We inched into the night
at sixty miles an hour, following
the limitations of an AM radio,
a metal dashboard, cracking vinyl,
the constant flapping of the wind
on the windows like tongues
crowded along the margin of glass
and vibrating invisibly, leering
at your hair hot-combed to silkiness
and lacking only the fateful gardenia
or my caress. The population of men
played in my ear.

Not even the studied putrefaction onstage
with the rock idol waltzing through
on drugs, a senile composer traversing
the broken glass of failed notes
as silence fell to dust,
not even the loud but limp music
could unlock my eyes as you
betrayed my innocent approbation
and clung to the arms of athletes
and negotiators whose suits
hung on them like the bright tenor
of roses, not dull and unwilling
like mine.
           "Hey boy, you want my phone number?"

No matter that I brought you here
and you left me, no matter
that I struggled to remember
a whole other song by a woman,

one who looked adoringly and sincerely
into my eye from the voyeurism
of television, no matter
that I knew in all my naïveté
that I was naïve and nothing
was of consequence as the world
expected nothing of me but
my attempt to consummate with you,
on one night, months of dreaming,
despite your indifference.

> "It's the little man in the boat.
> You don't know who he is,
> you don't know nothing!"

Coming back to the circle of men,
breathless, I had to explain
how you eluded me, how your
nakedness blinded me as I ran,
lunging after you with hands
filled with an apocryphal music
and the weight of erections,
whispering to myself,
> "This is not the prize."

patting the metal dashboard,
bellowing a dissonant love ballad,
meeting the spell of your breath,
wondering about the cymbal and brush
that is the cool temper and skin
of initiations and hunting,
the slick clicking of locks
in doors shutting in my face,
as refusal ran in rivulets
across your smile.

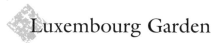Luxembourg Garden

for Danielle Legros Georges

I am set off
from men and women
by their tongues,
my brown-red skin,
their words I hear,
but am only learning
to speak, by a music
I am listening to,
for understanding. Nature
has caught me here,
in trees, sections
of grass, neatly laid
rows of plants. I have
been freed by language
to think how much there
is in the eye of a pigeon
that looks like me, black
and ploughing through
a thousand pat assumptions.
I set my croissants down
beside me, cover the juice
to keep out the leaves.
Thousands and thousands,
a universe of nerves
are placed on my every move—
from the leaves in trees,
from the blades of grass,
from the squirrels holding
me at bay. I am coming
to an early peace, the one
given when everything

familiar is taken away.
We see the plan of life.

This bench is on earth
owned once by the Medicis.
I watch the police in
their crisp blue, guarding
the grass. Nothing matters.

Stations in a Dream

1993

after Marc Chagall's Oeuvre

The Poet Reclining

I can never convince my father
that my best work is done in naps,
in the greenest of grass, near the smell
of manure, in the song of neighing
and snorting, in the infinite music
that fills the word with bright meaning.

After I am half out of life,
I can have discourse with the trees,
with each leaf that tickles itself,
and flirts with the branch, sending
me the secrets of a woman,
of the distinguishing flurry of her smile.

In this grass I always dream that
if I stay a little longer I will leave
this skin, skull, heart, brain,
femur, and blood, and melt into the soil
and multiply like the infinite beads
of this planet, becoming the thing
I spend my life singing to.

But I cannot convince my father,
who uses manure, tearfully, for flowers,
hoping to raise my mother
from her berth in the earth.

 Self-Portrait

I see myself in the shadows of a leaf
compressed to the green blades growing
to a point like the shards of miles of mirrors
falling and cracking to perfect gardens.

I never inspect the withered assumption
of my face's petty dialogue in raindrops,
the deceptive spreading of the words
oozing from the skin to the edges of water
etched on the ground by gravity and wishing.

Passing for the seriousness of my eye,
platitudes of my white collar or
the perfect posture of my lips, it skirts
from the leaves of the plant hiding me
and sits stoic like stone in my pupil,
mute and unassuming, like Rashi.

To gather myself I will swim naked
in the wind, bending my blind elbows
in circles, stopping now to dance
like the cherubic gold on the ark,
and gather myself from the particles
of this excitement another structure,
one closely resembling the beginning.

The Tree of Life

On the day we married, wholeness reigned,
music sprang from the full bud of a man
like a flower flying above the synagogue,
a presumptuous rooster pranced in the clouds.
The tree of life arose in its perfection
as large and beckoning as the sun, and
miracles worked their small fingers
in our ears, tickling and becoming.
Wishes we made as children turned incarnate,
the fruit of the trees was succulent,
not false or admonishing, and we were filled
with the sudden light like vessels crafted
by nimble hands just for that second.
We tasted wisdom and it has enriched us,
fed our hearts to bursting, set our souls
to dancing on the strings that bind the dream.

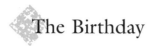# The Birthday

Your heart and mine are too different,
one a bickering roustabout that lounges
in the company of old men,
the other a yellow prodigy
that flies dutifully into the sun.

As bouquets are for wishing,
I have turned my spine inside out,
brought you one despite my indulgence,
my preference for lewd songs and laughter,
obeying the omens I have ignored
all my life, my blessed life, my dogged life.

You are imperturbable, cruising to the sun,
believing once there you can touch me
with a finger flaming and aloft,
set the lattice of my brain aright,
bring me to your room to lie down
and join the carnival of the city,
be at ease with life's creak and groan.
I celebrate your birthday with consenting.

My whispers want you to know
we are getting on, the light is dimming,
the night sounds are only life letting life.

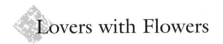

Lovers with Flowers

Can you contain my most intimate whisper,
settle it down after it has entered you,
make it a part of you and still cling
to my hand as gently as your eyes hold me?

Something must protect our weakness,
our mortality, and I choose the petal
and the leaf for their own transience,
as life is emboldened by mortal fear.

In this light through this glass and wood,
I sleep confidently in your murmurs and dreams,
deaf to significance, delighting
in our petty island of flowers and silences.

You have turned my soul to blazing pith.

Solitude

Alone I meditate on the invisible,
the potentially beautiful and minute chasms
of meaning that divide me and God,
the trailing words from his mouth
whose echoes taunt me with suggestions
of the Oral Torah, the grand perfection
before the first droplet of water,
or the setting of the first grain of sand.
Inside I listen for him to enter me,
to flow into this infinite cavern of my heart
and help me know this quiet village
behind me and the solitary angel above,
as other sanctities beg in my shadow,
offering foreign altars and hymns.

Adam and Eve

The serpent had an agent,
a tiny stag with a bird perched
on antlers that shone like silver,
suggesting flight to Eve, soaring
above the tree with its blue leaves,
going into the giant bass of God.
Adam was proud of his wife and the tree,
admiring the gesticulating trunk,
laughing at the snake's ludicrous dancing
like a drunken emperor. Before the fruit,
they held knowledge suspect,
but had no warning of the truth—
of life's prescience and power to transform.
Eve wept at the beauty of the faces in shadows.

# Bathsheba

Not even white dresses, fresh blossoms
or the despairing angels hovering could change
the fire that seized you the night after
she was through her period and her womb
lay open and fertile, beckoning you,
arousing you, leading like a siren.

Not all the concubines combined could deter
the beckoning of history, not even the memory
of how Michal saved your life could break the trance
of Bathsheba as you saw her bathing and allowed lust
to set your breath and soul on fire,
until there could be no euphony but your body with hers

emitting the percussion and wail of passion,
until you could have her beneath you, her eyes
widened and brightened by your driving sin.
And when death seemed the answer, you dispatched
it with all the authority of God's king,
all the madness and delirium of greed and guilt.

You chose your love from forbidden quarters,
and Solomon's soul sang in the marrow of your bones.

David

In your old age you adored the lyre.
All the women and all the births
were one wavering image, your trembling body
kept warm by a beautiful girl
you could only turn your eyes to and smile,
caress with the weak hands of a father.

A boy's ambitions can end in dreaming,
or they can be applauded by God
and given the power of metamorphosis,
changing like the angelic host from
wisp and mist to flesh, blood, stone,
wood, and fire—to life's stock.

You looked at Abishag, at her unblemished
figure, the soft call of her curling lips,
the dark hair falling on your shoulder
as she massaged your rigid neck
and rubbed her thighs against yours
to keep the king immortal, but desire was gone.

You remembered the countless marriages, the children,
wondered, without love, how could you have dreamed.

The Praying Jew

Seven severe indications of my love for you
were in the wall, flaming like the aura
around the temple at Sinai, speaking
in voices ranging to the imperceptible,
the invisible soprano of hosannahs,
of manna falling like walls of rain at night,
and I awake grasping for your embrace.

Walk with me past the dropping of the moon,
to where we inhabit the ocean and
our sojourn is through the cold timber
of my heart, to its center where you
can kiss it and set the world to beginning,
to creating and recreating itself infinitely,
to its center where I will vanish with you.

Hear my soul singing to you, shouting to me,
shimmering like the blinding vision of Ezekiel,
streaming down like the Oral Torah,
from your tongue to the Earth, to hearing.
Hear my soul reaching back to the full cloth
of your breath that rendered it to me.
Hear my prayer of desire for divine love.

Timber & Prayer
the
Indian Pond Poems

....

1995

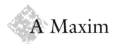# A Maxim

for Kala Weaver

I was once accused
of being a perfectionist.
In fact, she said
I tried to be
too perfect, as
just perfect was
not bad enough.
I was secretly proud
of the perfection
of someone who is
too perfect.
The greater secret
was I often felt
that I was unfinished,
just short of the mark.
The mark was always
moved by some manipulator.
After all, this sacred self,
the Hindu brilliant jewel,
is so, so subjective.
This person who
hung my guilt for
all the world to see
probably just saw in me
something she wanted.
For us perfect folk,
all life coheres.
We are secret egotists.
We worship curves,
the round parts
that make life
more interesting.

The curves are where
mistakes are taken
lightly, taken out
of guilt's crucible.
In perfection,
the perfect wash
themselves in shame,
as my brilliant jewel
catches me smiling
in its perfect mirrors.

The Final Trains of August

for Michael S. Harper

He stands in the unfinished door
of his antique shop, above Bar Harbor.
He leans on the sill to relieve
his trick knees, watches
the final trains of August,
vacationers with their bicycles
on the tops of RVs and minivans,
teenagers with their feet propped
in the window. They mimic
some abandon coined a long way off.
He counts the possible customers,
the accountants from Boston
with their neat wives who move
through his collection smug and sure,
like necromancers who make money
out of the sagacious purchase,
or the infrequent Southerners
who betray summers of the South
for the cool nights and mountains
of Maine with its wilderness
and its infinite lay of lakes.
He watches and imagines
what stragglers will land
in his world of sundry history.

"I want a window," she says,
and Walter announces himself.
He holds out his pearl-white beard,
"Walter Francis, retired colonel
and antique trader at your service."
"I want a window," she repeats.
He takes her into the basement,

past some yellow Jehovah's Witness
books spread in a basket,
past the collection of chairs
where people had their breakfast
or where they watched the chill
of autumn come in with full colors.
They move past tables where folks served tea
to neighbors who passed time with grace,
past the baby scale where doctors
held protesting children to see
how much they had grown back
before the electronic scale and Similac.
They reach the old windows.
Her face breaks open and brightens.
"Where is this from, what time,
what house?" She presses her palm to a pane.
"Ma'am, I get these windows
from all over this region and beyond."
She persists, prodding on,
"What house, what house is this?"
He pulls the suspenders holding him,
"Ma'am, this was a quiet house,
off to itself, where the rain
beat like light fingers on a drum."
She takes it quickly, writes
the check in tight, even letters,
announces that she is an artist.
Walter lights a Marlboro.
"I get them all," he muses,
"everybody comes to Walter Francis."

"Gertrude and I built this place,"
he tells a couple from Hartford.
Gertrude walks across the road.
"She runs the motel and I run
this fabulous collection of the old."

Gertrude reaches them, moves
as easy as a teenager with legs
long and supple as they were
when she was an Air Force lieutenant
to Walter's Vietnam colonel.
They believed that nothing
but the end could stop them,
the end that comes to all of us,
and to everything we own,
the end that falls to the care in
hands of angels and preservationists.
She reaches them, speaks loudly,
"Walter, I'm gonna unload that truck.
It'll be dark soon, too dark to work."
He growls softly, "Gertrude,
get on back to the motel. Go on."
She ignores him, moves to the truck, tosses
in the new antiques like a stevedore,
things new to this way station
of the old but unforgotten.
"That woman thinks she's my boss,
after I took this business
to be rid of the overseers, the judges."
The young couple ponder
a relay box from the 1880s,
precisely kept in a wooden cabinet,
polished, tightened, and smoothed.
They decline and move out
into the brisk air of the evening,
to make the night drive to Hartford.

The last stranger fills the threshold,
a young man who travels alone. He is
up from Providence to see the mountain
of the Roosevelts, Cadillac Mountain,
where F.D.R. came to forget

the weight of guiding America.
The stranger considers
buying an old-fashioned life preserver
made of tamarack wood.
Walter takes his cue to land
a lecture on the origin of his house,
built in the eighteenth century
by a man who built frigates and schooners
for a living. Walter explains the house
is a seagoing vessel, tight and solid.
He could lift it and move it
today and not even disturb it.
The nursery floor is tamarack
because that kept life's noise at bay.
The house has outlived endings.
The stranger pushes his fingers
into the night air, marvels
at the stars. Walter reminisces
about the Orient where he wondered
if adventure lay in what the dead
leave behind. In the sick humidity
of Vietnam, he made a regular route
to our last heralded door and stopped
just short of hearing the answers.
The stranger from Providence
coughs to break the meditation
and then climbs roughly into
an old Chevrolet with scabs of rust.
He drives away toward the ocean.

Walter hobbles on his trick knees,
turns off the lights, closes down
the shop with its unfinished walls.
At the road's edge, he lights a Marlboro,
blows the smoke ahead, walks into it,
as he listens to the regrets of the dead.

Mass Transit

for Sonia Sanchez

She sat at the front
near the driver, watched
as new riders dropped
their change and flashed passes.
She sat stoical and grim
in a dress blue like the passive
colors for a baby boy,
or the blue of peace.
Everyone jostled along
with the creak and moan
of the bus that strained
to fit the contours of earth
like a worm in a straitjacket.

I peeked over the shoulder
of the woman in front of me
to read her Haitian newspaper.
I caught the bold print
in an ad for a get-rich scheme—
Devenez riche maintenant!
She read slowly and intently,
while the rest of us ached
silently for a quiet ride home.
In all this intimacy, we were
thrown together with strangers:
grandmothers who returned
from shopping where merchants
devour the poor,
young women who carried books
home from college,
the community college
where they battled like Marines

for their hope, and me
with my briefcase and poetry,
as I rode back from the law school.
All of us ached
for a quiet ride home.

The woman in blue erupted
but did not change her face.
With the same smile
almost a grimace she said,
"Better get ready for the judgment,
my Lord is coming down."
The bus rattled
over a large pothole as
we all shot up stiffly for a second
and realized she was preaching.
"All this crack and stuff.
Lord don't like it! You all guilty!"
Suddenly she became
what I suspect she wanted to be,
the angel sent in the last hour
before the others come
with their wrecking crew
of pestilence, famine, and war.
They turn a perfect summer day
like this to burning blood
and raise the lake of fire
so that everyone can see
the serpent beat the surface
with his infinite tail.
Her blue became the blue
of some fires that look cool
from a distance, belie
their ability to make the skin
crackle and curl to ash.

The driver picked up speed,
hoped that each stop
would be hers and her sermon
would stop its march up and down
like a rider who intimidates
on the late-night buses,
when the angry old men ride.
But she sat as if riveted
to her seat. Slowly,
the passengers began to thank her
as they got off, those riders
who knew the hour of our condition.
They touched her softly on the knee
and whispered kindly to her,
"God bless you, sister."
She smiled and adjusted
her grip on her Bible.

We began to forget
about her and Judgment Day.
We bounced along, braced ourselves
for the awkward crawl
around the corners as we passed
the deserted lots of Newark
and headed into East Orange.
There men in disheveled clothes
gathered near abandoned buildings.
It seemed that doom
had already come with its heralds
and gone. Through it all
I thought of a friend's dispensation
for those travelling the Apocalypse—
"Only the poor ride the bus."

Going to Church with C. W.

We spellbind like the annunciation.
You amble over to your cane,
favor the leg that threatens to surrender.
I shuffle over to the cordless phone
to peek at the red recharging indicator.
Two cantankerous supplicants, we head
for a New England church, wooden and white,
an eightyish white woman with her companion,
a thirtyish black man with his diva.
We slip through the wet grass to worship.

Down the road, Jesus. Down the road to joy.
Shadows of the congregations of leaves
whip over the car like a lover's whine.
You ask me about the book I manage
barely to write, slowly, with pain.
You resurrect again your Radcliffe degree
in literature, your fondness for Victorian fiction.
I remind you of your rude impertinence,
how worship blurts out our duty
to be meditative, to acknowledge the splendor
of the sun's confident slide over the mountains,
of the minute splash of butterflies in the stream.

I come, Lord, come this way to please you.
We waddle into the temple. Floors creak,
heads turn, eyes spin, and mouths drop
as we go to the front pew. You fix
your eyes on your almost century of life,
from the roads, the dirt roads before the car
to the unmarked highway that leads to the moon.
I wonder how long I can stay in your grace,

how the separation will wake one sad day,
how we will find excuses to hurt each other.

Through the benediction and the hush,
we walk together outside, an unusual machine
turning on the pistons of forgiveness and curiosity.
Halfway home we stop at a store for ice cream.
You blink quickly over the dashboard.
I pay for our diversion. The clouds
suggest a thunder far away and above us
like the noise from flesh's integration
as our hearts circle one another and join.
The wind sticks wet lips to us as we drive home
to the squeak and creak of the colonial farmhouse,
up the winding path along the stone wall.
Hold my hand, Father. Hold my hand when I die.

My Son Flies to Visit Me in Providence

for Kala Weaver

You shot past the flight attendant
trying to look worldly, but for all
your sang-froid, you were quite askew.
Twelve and travelling alone,
your shirttail flapping out, collar
hanging over your jacket, buttons
misaligned, shoelaces flailing about.
You were quite terrified
of having flown this far with strangers.
We walked along slowly
through the airport as small
as a Kmart where passengers
dressed in jeans with cheap bags
waited for flights to the outer world.
They were refugees from the rustication
of Rhode Island with the Mafia,
and the international village of Providence.

I pointed out to you the hill
where the colonials fought back
the British, a hill owned by a slaver.
You were not impressed
by subtleties of lives lived and gone,
and wanted only to know why
at this juncture in your grand design
I had chosen to come here away
from everything we both knew.
I took away the tidy row house near the lake,
afternoons in your room with videos,
Sunday roar of fans from the stadium
where the Orioles lost game after game,
and the hikes through the park.

I remembered regretfully
that you left first, you smashed
the photograph of us standing together
and called your mother, and left.
What are children if they are not
conscious of what they do, even if
they cannot fully see the outcome?
Neither can we with our wealth
of mistakes. So in the vacuum
I left too, left everyone.
I left to recover something lost
long ago when I had more chances.
You wanted to know why
there was such pleasure for me
in a brick room full of books,
as you threw tantrums and begged
the impossible, to be readmitted
into my small space, to be relieved,
but on the last day I sent you back,
agreeing with your mother's wishes.
Sadly, I signed you over to the plane and
to the good graces of Eleanora, my first wife,
who waited, smiling, in our youth.

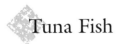Tuna Fish

for Lucille Clifton

Every day tuna fish,
in every conceivable manner.
With tomatoes that leaked
and made the bread soggy,
with lettuce my mother tore
in odd shapes that hung
like ornaments from my mouth
in the cafeteria, the high court.
I had tuna on toast toasted lightly
that was death-cold at noon,
on toast toasted darkly
that crumbled like old ruins
just when I was in front
of LaRue Ashe. She always
wanted to kiss me long
before I knew why she
was so proud of the French
in her name.

Tuna in waxed paper
that tore and fell on the floor,
tuna in aluminum foil
shaped like flying saucers
that we threw at each other
in assassination attempts.
Tuna from brand names,
Star-Kist that always rejected
hip Charlie in the sunglasses,
Bumble-Bee with its
oxymoron soul of insects and fish.
Tuna made the day before,
which seemed to smell

truly like dead fish, the dead fish
killed by pollution and washed up
like rejected never-to-be's,
the dead fish of hot sun.
And nothing was so obviously poor
as eating this when other kids
had hot spaghetti from the kitchen
where women like my mother
labored over shiny pots and steam.

Nothing was so distinctly humble
as munching tuna and mayo
when LaRue Ashe mounted
the bench of the table
like the acrobat she was
and asked aggressively for a kiss.
I sat as stupid
as a confused cat, blinked,
masticated the sea's journeyman,
bemoaned my banal lunch,
but dreaded the deeper pit
of despair, tuna's alter ego,
bologna. I knew full well
and grievously that LaRue
could never come to view
bologna as romantic. I knew
perhaps unconsciously that few
meats are as seductive as fish.

Sub Shop Girl

for James Mann

She is lovely. Her eyes are big almonds
floating over the electronic cash register.
She puts magic dust in my mayonnaise,
hoochie-koochie notes in my fries.
There is no other reason to order
tomatoes, lettuce, hot peppers, onions,
and french fries in a suit and tie.
I come nearer the shop tiptoeing in Florsheims.
With a quarter I set the mood on the jukebox.
"What do you want today?" she asks. "What is it, Baby?"
I am probably the only man who puts strategy
in a Saturday night foray to the sub shop.
I line my cologne up carefully on the dresser,
the Parisian designer bottle for cheese steak,
for pizza the cheaper, less subtle aromas,
laying my clothes out to match each meal.
She puts the change in my palm a coin at a time,
measuring the contours of the lines in my hands.
I think I lost my sanity a long time ago
on the way to buy a foot-long and fries.
The essence of Sango fires my red urge
longing to meld with the small greasy apron
that throws frozen steak portions with expertise.
How could the heavens have wasted such youth
on me and this corner sub shop and vagrants
and the empty neon in after-hours streets,
and the music from old Smokey Robinson 45s
I play on my boom box the nights I want to serenade?
Have you ever listed the extras on a cold cut with
"Tracks of My Tears" or "Second That Emotion"?

When the shop is closed some Sundays I melt
in the afternoon apparitions in the empty windows,
the deserted counters, the cold ovens, the silence.
There are blessings for noble spirits confined
to ordinary lives, the dribble of an oba like me
and a great spirit like my sub shop Osun slicing pickles.
There are blessings as we dazzle the ordinary universe,
pervert the threadbare perceptions of doldrums
with our elegant affair at night, our perfect love,
me in an all-leather racing jacket and Gucci loafers.

One night after work I'll coax her and we'll pretend
to be Marvin Gaye and Tammi Terrell on the parking lot.
I'll caress her around the waist and spin her softly.
A dark night sky laden with stars will crack,
the moon will pour love's essence on the earth,
truth will overcome us on the voices of the orisas—
"Ain't Nothing Like the Real Thing," or maybe
"You're All I Need to Get By," but most of all the song
the world needs to hear—"You Ain't Livin Till You're Lovin."
I am probably the only man who sees the answer
in a cheese-steak hoagie with all the fixins and fries,
music from my boom box or the jukebox nearby,
two almond eyes as deep as canyons over the counter,
and my Gucci and Florsheim shoes doing a soft tap,
the mania and danger of an insecure world hanging out
like a florid design in the curtain of the night.

Bootleg Whiskey for Twenty-five Cents

for Jaye T. Stewart

They lap up their liquor with virtuosity,
the stiff imports from Macon, Georgia,
the velvet brand from Memphis, Tennessee,
the West Indian cool from Florida.
They sway together upstairs at Jackie's.
They listen to Duke on the radio. Codas
coddle the heads on necks of putty
that taste jazz with home brew and sodas.

Their new shoes are from downtown
with Italy stamped inside. Their dresses
came to them from full closets where a frown
from wealth shines down. The city confesses
to ballrooms where corn liquor is thrown down
like New York water. A few undress,
love. They can't do better or worse. The gown
of gaiety envelops them, possesses.

They debate the undebatable. They drift away,
in Jackie's back room, in syncopated sway.

Talisman

·······················

1998

# The Robe

Mama and her sisters
were dancing in the living room,
cackling, bending the floor.
I was downstairs in the tub,
scrubbing my knees with Ajax,
wondering where the black
came from, where it went.
I was afraid to cross
the living room sea of women
with their party, afraid of what
I did not know of women,
their delight in measuring
the sex of naked little boys.
They prophesied a boy's
potential to please a woman
by studying hairless dicks.
Afraid more of being late for bed
than of being seen, I put on
my yellow robe. I wrapped myself
like a fireman about to enter
a burning building, and I climbed
the stairs where my mother
stood with her mischievous smile.
I walked into this room of women
who loved me, and my mother
pulled off my robe for all to see
what kind of man I could be.
Shame cut me like a cleaver.
Once in a nightmare, I saw
my mother at the top of the stairs,
face raging, hair full like Medusa,
daring me to climb, daring me.

Michele

My baby sister used to get
her baths on the kitchen sink.
We were in our new house
in a neighborhood where white folk
used to live, but they left fast.
Everybody was colored now,
and we did colored kinds of things,
like bathing babies in the kitchen.
That's the first I remember Michele,
brown and naked up on the counter
in that little, plastic baby tub.
She had her legs up in the air,
feet kicking around, smiling.
I tiptoed on nine-year-old feet
and looked all over this baby sister.
I looked between her legs
for a long time, just a studying.
Her pee hole looked like a keyhole.
Mama said all girls was like that,
and I knew what boys had because
I was a boy. I had questions.
"Mama, if that is a keyhole,
what is the key? Where is the door?
What house is we in anyway?"

Humility

Mama knew when I was a baby
that I was arrogant, a sweet
little boy but full of pride.
A man came with a camera when
I was just three and took pictures
of me and Cousin Bonita.
I sat up with my legs crossed,
looking just like the prince I was.
I had a lot of heart, like boys
used to say about courage.
My first-grade teacher said
I was a born leader, I had something
that made it easy for me to be
in control of a situation.
Mama kept telling me I had
to be humble in this life,
so I hid this power of mine
behind smiles and knew in secret
that I was the smartest boy
in the world. Some part of me
wanted to seize life, and some part
was afraid of what life would seize in me.
Mama mixed things up sometimes,
saying be humble and then be a man.
Like the time this girl tried
to beat up my sister Marva who I was
supposed to protect. I just stood
while the girl cussed my sister out,
but she didn't hurt Marva. I knew
this girl wasn't nothing but mouth,
But Mama got mad at me for not
beating this girl out there in the alley.

Mama was always mixing me up,
and I knew I had to do what she say.
So I went in my room and felt guilty
for not smacking this girl in the face.
I thought about what I should have done,
and my anger got bigger and bigger.

Mama made up her courage.
She was always mouthing off about
what she would do to somebody.
I was going to a white school then,
and I wanted to tell Mama bout herself,
bout the ways of the white man's world.
Mr. Charlie let black girls scream and cuss
all they want to, all the damn day long,
but he dares black boys to say a word,
a mumbling word, or he will kill us.

Writing Numbers

She decided to go in business,
get herself some paper and pencils,
talk on the phone all morning.
Everything was figures,
dreams, sales receipts, voices
from the television and radio,
radio preachers with secret codes.
On Friday evenings, Mister Joe
would come, this scroungy-looking
white man with a bulge in his jacket.
Mama would give him papers
and some money. She got to keep
some of it. Aunt Peaches was in business
right along with Mama, both of them
talking about three-digit numbers.
Once, Aunt Peaches had to go to jail
to speak on this business of hers
and Mama's, and Mama panicked.
She wrapped up all her numbers
in little bits of aluminum foil
and froze them in the freezer.
Them numbers couldn't go nowhere.
They was stuck in ice and couldn't
combinate themselves or repeat or nothing.
She didn't stay in business
with numbers after this. She did hair.
Later on Mama told me that bulge
in Mister Joe's jacket was a gun.

Mt. Zion Baptist

Before Grandma couldn't walk,
we all went to church together sometimes.
We sat in one little group on the pew
like the pictures of black folk
on the backs of the fans we used
to cool ourselves in the church.
Mama wanted me to always do things
like they supposed to be done.
Her word for right was *businessfied*.
Even now when I am making love,
the woman gotta know I'm *businessfied*.
The singing was usually good,
and I knew all about this church.
I was in Sunday School and on
the Junior Usher Board.
I went to Baptist Training Union.
One Sunday in winter we went
to morning service, and I got bored.
I was getting to be fifteen,
feeling like a man, smelling my pee,
as Mama and her sisters called it.
So I put my hands behind my head
in church and closed my eyes.
I didn't want to hear that mess
the pastor was dragging out himself.
We went home and Mama told me
to go in the back room and take
my clothes off and get ready for a beating.
I took off everything except my underwear
and waited for her. She came in
like the roll of thunder and beat me.
I cried the cry of shame. I wanted Daddy

to come and save me. Mama had
gone stone crazy on my behind.
When she knew she was dying,
Mama apologized to me.
It was spring. I was thirty years old.

Mama's Hoodlum

The summer
out of high school,
I started drinking and
hanging out with tough boys.
I carried a knife cause
we didn't bother much
with guns. The older, tougher
men had Roscoes of
various calibers. I drank
Thunderbird and Pineapple Richard's
cause they was less than
a dollar for a whole fifth.
The next day your head felt
like it was slapped against
the Grand Canyon. We raced
my father's car and almost
killed ourselves quite a few times.
We threatened people
and was generally thought
to be a gang. We was Big Time
in Baltimore. Some of my boys
shot up heroin and smoked reefer.
One night I got so high
my friends dumped me on my porch.
Mama opened the door,
and I fell into the living room,
rolling around like a seal.
I was wrestling with my manhood.
Mama went for my wallet,
and I stood up as if to hit her.
Daddy jumped up like Joe Louis,
and I was bout to cry but I broke

for the back door and disappeared.
Daddy tried to follow me
in his car I used for racing,
but I hid in a friend's house.
Then I jumped in a cab and
went to Danny's house, where
I slept. Danny's father was
the president of Coppin State College.
Cousin Geff brought me home
the next day after I called
from Uncle Geth's to apologize.

There was nothing like being high,
feeling brave, having the respect
of other boys who swore to die for me.
"Mike, man, I would go down for you."
Music like *Junior Walker and the All-Stars*
playing "I'm a roadrunner, Baby.
Can't stay in one place too long,"
while I raced city streets at seventy
miles per hour in summertime.
Being bad felt so good and right
while Mama sat home and worried
about how and when I might die.

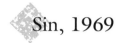

Sin, 1969

It was better
than anything I had
ever done in
my whole life.
We took our clothes
off in a bedroom
in Aunt Grace's house
when the grownups
was gone. I looked
at your golden brown
skin near yellow,
and your titties full
and the thick bush
of hair on your pussy.
I was charged
like electric had
taken over my blood.
We made love
without even thinking
about making a baby.
We walked outside.
It was a sunny day.
I could feel the heat
in my chest cause
it was sticking out.
I wondered why anybody
would want this
to be a sin.

The Incomplete Heart

When my son was born retarded,
Mama forgot she had begged me
to get an abortion and send this boy
back to God. He had Down's Syndrome,
complete with a heart that was without
a wall between the lower chambers.
His blood ran through his body
without proper direction, like love.
One morning he did not wake up,
after the daily rushes to the hospital,
after ten months of trying to live,
of smiling when I tickled him but
not being able to sit up or develop.
I went with my wife to a department store
to buy his funeral outfit. We was just
children our damn selves, just children,
and we had to bury this first son
we had named a junior. At the funeral,
his mother tried to take him out
of the casket, and we had to pull
her back and make her sit down.
Girl, let the dead go, let him go.

I cried a little but mostly was a man,
until a year later when I drove
through the city, chased by police
at high speed from the cemetery.
I was on the television and everything.
They had me in chains, and I crawled
over to Mama and cried on her knees.
I had gone insane. I wanted to forget

the power was given to God,
who had took my son and my mind.

Friendship, 1994

Companion friends love each other.
—Laurence Thomas

I stayed away
for two months, caught up
in myself, wondering
if we were friends. The day
I came back *Sango* was
making thunder over us.
I could see myself
in things I mailed to you.
We walked to *Mitali's*.
I followed, afraid
of my anger and yours.
In the rain, stepping sideways,
we went for another Indian lunch.
I was beginning to see
my love was my first love
rising again from its grave.
With a doggy bag, we walked
to Sixth Avenue, went over reviews
of *Alma's Rainbow*, your film.
We parted, you with the food,
your feet in black sneakers.
At Penn Station I got lost in
the chatter of commuters.
I grabbed my New York *Post*
for the gossip, bought a bottle
of water. It wasn't my grief,
my offering of gifts to you, *Osun*,
to set your soul aflame. No,
my loneliness was all over me,
a new temple over this body,
my own demons. Train stations

are where I feel the exchange
of life's weight, spirit to spirit.
Time has a gift that is not time.

House Training

Every Saturday morning,
I got up before everybody else,
everybody except her.
She always had one eye open.
With my bucket and my rags,
I cleaned the kitchen and
the rest of the basement, scrubbing
the yellow walls that are still
yellow after forty years.
Scraping and rubbing, I got
the black-and-white kitchen floor
so bright the tiles shined when
I put on the liquid wax. I had
the bathroom looking like a picture.
Mama was proud of me, and
she talked with her sisters about
how nice I did everything. I could cook.
I could wash clothes and iron, too.
One day one of Mama's sisters said,
"Michael sure will make some girl
a mighty fine husband, mighty fine."
Only God and Mama knew the truth—
Mama was preparing me to be alone.

New Poems

The Black and White Galaxie

for Gene F. Thomas

With water warm enough to make me
feel the gust of spring color,
I added dish detergent and a rag.
The rag was soft enough to caress her
but raise the dirt from her skin.
The soap was strong yet weak so
it wouldn't make her complexion crack.
Then I started at the top of her,
scrubbing the roof of the Ford Galaxie,
my Uncle Frank's cruising machine.
When he trusted me, he watched me
from afar. Then he let me go alone,
having given me a tenet of his wisdom—
a black man gotta make his car shine.

I knew how to hold the water hose,
spray it so it came out in a shower.
I chased the bubbles away and over her,
until the white was like a star's smile,
and the black seemed to pull me into it.
Thru the rolled up windows, I checked
the preliminaries, the interior,
an intimate space of hushed conversations,
smiles, and hands on thighs in corners
after bars closed, of lipstick,
of the black woman's accoutrements.
I checked to see if it was clean enough
to hail a woman's aloof eyes and lips.
Uncle Frank told me what women want—
a black man gotta look like money.

The tires were the last, but I saved
a tough energy for them. In motion,
a car's wheels are the signals of the way
its soul hisses, sucks in its breath.
It breathes air like that spring air
of purple and yellow when I washed
the first car I ever drove, as Uncle Frank
let me turn it around in the alley.

I dreamed of chasing women with a machine
that could play music and smell like evergreens.
I dreamed of the hunt and being in the cut.
Uncle Frank threw in *men's mother wit*
to keep me out of Baltimore's apocalypse—

a black man gotta wear suits and ties,
a black man gotta have a private world.

Inside the Blues Whale

1978–1979
for Vincent Woodard

It is not just my problem. It belongs
to us all. I have been cajoled into
coming to the emergency room where
everything scares me. Black folk
shoot and cut each other until they end
here where guards have guns. I refuse
to be taken upstairs and locked away.
I was trying to think of a poem. It got me
to this place. With my mother, I stand
against the wall, guards on either side.
They have guns, and this is my mother.
It is now everybody's problem. A bird
is singing in my hair, more important
than Thorazine. My head is a tree
stretching its leaves to burn in the sun.
They say if I make a treaty to take
the medicine, I can leave with my family
since my family is crazy. I look at the guns
on the hips of the guards and know I must
be as still and quiet as death or this will
turn into psychosis as sick as nightmares.
I am angry that they would have me here
with my mother, angry at white doctors.
I am in a whale in the ocean. Who can
swim out to me? Who can cast a line?
If I take out the first guard by breaking
his neck, I can protect my mother, but
it is more important that we are all now
underwater, inside a whale who laughs.
Later the therapist they say likes me
keeps talking about the appointment.

She is doing something subliminal with
the word "come," repeating, repeating.
She leans to me when she says it.
It bothers me that such people think
crazy people are stupid, but it is more
important that my head is a tree
with a bird singing in it inside a whale
in the ocean. The most important thing
of all is that this whale that ate us
likes to laugh a lot. He has the blues.

Abiku

for Michael S. Weaver, Jr. 1971–1972

The only way to chase ghosts is in the tub.
I close the bathroom door and let the room
fill with steam. My mind wiggles open.
I put music on my head to seal the world
inside me and flush out infecting spirits.
I touch hurt that is twenty-three years old,
the cold potato feel of your body in the coffin
like a toy. I touch the day I went mad with
grief at your fresh grave, see the night's sky
as I rode to Crownsville State Hospital.

If I had not fathered you before marriage,
if I had not thought you would make me a man,
if I had not forgotten children's suffering,
if I had not taken this road to madness,
what road would there have been for me?
Count my gifts to you—ten months of life,
my name engraved in bronze in the earth.

Kings

for David Johns

This woman is a stranger,
a tall brunette born the same year
as your first son. With lubricant,
she pushes the catheter in the canal
of your old penis, to release the water.
She asks if it hurts, and you
grasp the sheets, stare at the ceiling.
The Lord turns the king's heart . . .

They have cloned a sheep.
It stares from TV without recognition
of the Earth, not sure it has landed,
caught too much in professional care,
like this quiet linen of a place
that denies endings. I see you,
my father's nakedness, the urge
that imagined me inside an orgasm.

Your pain, your shame collide
in my hands hung over the arms
of the chair. The catheter fails.
You are too full, and she wheels you
into the shower for the inspiration
of water falling. Piss, and live.

I listen, the seas spitting life, gift
of you & my mother. O, Jordan.

Lamentations #1

If only my soul were a messy garage
outside the house I have always wanted.
Then I would be a pile of fenders,
old tires and engine parts, carburetors on
shelves, wrenches everywhere, buckets of dirty oil,
some skeleton of a car in the middle with old
lawnmowers. It would be a tinker's joy, you
in the corner there, sitting beside me, the two
of us not quite finished, not joined with wires
that pull the current around, make the lights go.
I could go over to you, shuffle over, step
in puddles of grease and grime, follow the squeak
of your voice like the up and down of old springs.

Putting your parts with my parts, we look
like the working thing that we should be.
Sputtering, we come to life, and this stumbling
mechanic we have been for so long falls into
a pile of bolts, wires, nuts, panels, and grease.

He sleeps while you and I resurrect
him whole and full. Then we die again,
fall back into the incompleteness. Back
and forth this goes, until in one realization
a brand-new car rolls out of the garage.

We sit in it, me driving, adjusting the radio,
with a license plate saying "Father and Son."

Lamentations #2

In the basement of Johns Hopkins hospital,
Mama's body rested on the steel table. Steel
is more convenient because you can wash away
the blood and scraps. A hole was in her neck
where they had tried to put her on a machine,
but she would not stay. She left us with the trace
of a smile on her face with white frost on her lips.
Gone. So gone that the place was filled with her.

You took her wedding band from her fingers
and walked down the hall until you burst like
a humid cloud or pig belly. Then you started
talking to me out of the silence of my whole life,
out of all the years I watched you half in fear,
like the time I came home drunk and screamed
at Mama as if I was gonna hit her. Out into
the dark I ran away from what I did not know
of you, your big hands, the way you look
like a desperate old lion sometimes, the kind
that kill out of a fear of their own sons, of death.

You haven't stopped talking. I still wonder
what there is to say. So many years and now
I am this friend when all your friends are dying.
My friends are dying, too, or is it that I pick
friends with so much to give in so little time?

I played the piano once after Mama died.
Once you said "I can see you on the saxophone."
How do you know these secrets?
What key is in this small silence left to us?

Lamentations #3

In the last years, sweetness is a growl,
the way you summon laughter from fussing
at this and that. The other night I heard you
thinking of Uncle Richard, his gangsta belly,
the sharp gleam of his switchblades.
Trade the nothing howl of watching wrestling
alone to laugh/be with this brother-in-law
who is dead. Give it back for a minute of life
more like it was than what it has become.

In the kitchen, your hands in the water,
you snarl at your grandchildren and they laugh
to see you laugh, walking from side to side,
trading ache for ache, wiping the table clean
of crumbs from children's cereal, toast
broken into bits. The clap of a pan
is the echo where you hear wailing,
all alone in the need of prayer. We descend
in circles to where we breathe, and we return,
some of us believing. We return and leave
the difficulty of shopping alone for groceries
to those who know complaint, who know
how to hope for the rising in the morning.

The family's men turn brittle, become
dust, go grunting, leave behind the task
of setting bears to run in your laughter.
I stare down your fear, dare it to break,
chase your dust's endless roll, fading into
the danger of a car overturned in a river,
lullabies in leaves as you rise, Canaan's son.

Lamentations #4

I was a father for you in the few years
before I had a son. In my hospital stays,
I failed you like a hero will when you see
his scars, the way he tries to undo
accumulated pain in the morning. I tell
our father to limber up in the mornings,
come into some kind of fluidity that was
taken for granted when he was as young
as I am, but I feel old. I can't play
basketball with you for long because
of this left ventricle, a sound like vehicle—
Pontiac, Chrysler, Chevrolet, Buick.

That day we played Monopoly.
You were nine or ten, with skateboards
and sweatbands. You surprised me,
cried in your arms. There was something
I should have done. It doesn't matter.
I can't buy property in this crowded tear.

Lamentations #5

The puppeteer is distracted,
excited by a fire on the edge,
and you collapse. In the bathroom,
in the dark, alone in the house,
your head misses cracking the bowl.
"Scramble," is all you can think,
"scramble like some last chance."
Grab what you can while the house
is falling down, and when it has fallen,
love the earth, stay close to it.
Crawl like a seventy-four-year-old
newborn adam who can't remember
his mother's tit or how to cry
out loud from her swollen vagina.

The carpet makes a nuisance
of a scratching. "Pull," you think,
"pull yourself into the damn bed."

Body, don't fuck up on me now.
O, my sweet Lord, pick up the strings.

Radio Days

for Mark J. Weaver

My father has a picture of me
taken around the time Charlie Parker
died. I am sitting up like a prince,
erect, bright, smiling. I have promise
around my head woven in vines
of gold, but this is not in the picture.
I remember radio from then,
checking the paper for my shows.

My father had a habit of bringing
home toys to me, small things on days
he got paid. It was a reward
for being firstborn and being a son.
I was supposed to make the future
a safe place. I had to kill the lion.

I look at my son and my brother.
I look at my father. The four of us
are a circuit where the current is
a stream of hope & fear, floating,
going back, living and not living.

We hold up our hands and dreams
fly out of them, birds of blue electric.

The Poets

1965–1968

In the gymnasium the balls spun
from their fingers like spiders' silk,
fine and unconquerable. Legs woven
in threads of hope, they jumped,
came down on silent sneakers,
dashing any hopes we had of winning.
They were the blacks, the black blacks
who had the advantage of being born.

Dunbar, the high school that sent
a jingle in a broken tongue to colleges
on full scholarships. Dunbar, the high
school that we watched march here
to smash us once again, we black boys
with all these white boys too thick
to dance like a knife in the air,
to open, cut, slice a tangled history.

Breath held back "nigger" in the air
over the bleachers. Breath held back
"wino junkies" under the old clock
over the hollering wooden floor where
we sang pep songs in German, peeping
inside our shirts and ties at our own
magic. The Dunbar Poets made baskets
while strolling, dreaming of rivers.

"Coach, we can't do nothing with
these darkies from Dunbar. Coach,
their bodies ain't bodies. They are
songs from somewhere unfair to us."
We, the black folk at Polytechnic,

107

wished from the white sea of equality
that Dunbar would stamp blackness
all over this stiff building to save us.

The lead opened so wide it was
too hard for The Poets to keep from
laughing. They slapped their hands
and did the slow jazz of black boys
walking away from an easy game.
In the streets, we watched them stride
away in Florsheims to get high,
too brilliant to live, too brilliant to die.

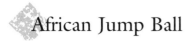

African Jump Ball

for E. Ethelbert Miller

Can you dribble? Aw man, you can't dribble.
Do you know travelling ain't going to the West Side
    to see your woman?
Dribble, man! This ain't no Amtrak Metroliner!
Don't bogarde me, trying to roll off to the left.
Your layup ain't that tough. Don't try the sky hook.
Give me that ball, partner. Give me that ball.
                    This is *friendship one on one.*
I'll cut you some slack. Go back to half court
and just run here to the foul line. Do a jumper.
I'll even let you do a set shot and won't even smack
it back to where you buy them dirty sneakers
every Saturday, the *You Was Here Yesterday Store.*
Tell you what. We'll play for African-American Trivia.
Tell me when William Wells Brown stopped running.
            I'll spot you six points.
This one is even better. Who is bigger and what
the hell is the big that they got? Chamberlain or Jabbar?

You sweatin, man. See, you sweatin. I ain't
busted a bead nowhere, as dry as when my honey
wiped me down this morning with that terry towel
and called me love, called me sweetness.
You and me got trickster hearts,
but I know a foul ain't no fried chicken, cuz.
        Bert, enough with the bum rush, man.
        See there, we done set the net on fire.

Eighteen

for Honorée Fanonne Jeffers

The overhead crane operator starts
his monster my way. It is three stories
tall and yellow and clicking sparks.
I check my chicken I have on the heater,
wrapped in aluminum foil, and I put on
my gloves. Everything around me
is grease and oil. Everything is dirt.
The crane is above me, and I hook it
to the new steel rolls for the tin mill.
I could lose my hand anywhere here,
in the steel coupling, in the cables.
I go on silent faith, knowing my job.

There are so many ways to get maimed
or to die here. Underground one time
I worked handling scrap tin in a bin.
It came twisting down from above me.
If I got caught in the flow, I could have
been dragged to the machine that winds
and be wound flat until my head popped
like an orange. These tin mills
are bombs. One day one exploded.
Nothing was left but a black skeleton.

I am eighteen years old, and I write poems
on the backs of tally sheets for the tin.
I read Du Bois and James Weldon Johnson.
The white men hate me. The black men
don't trust me. I have fourteen years
of this ahead of me, in another factory.
There I will break rules to read books.
At lunch time, I pull my fried chicken

off the heater and get coffee to rinse
the soot down my throat. I listen.
Steel is an orchestra inside a cave.
I listen. I hear a prison's hollowing.

Enemies

At night the loading-dock doors are open
to the truckyard. The church sits in the middle,
defiant and mostly empty. They would rather
worship once a month in silence than sell
to the company so that trucks can swing
around without cursing church and chapel.
It is quiet, nowhere the howling and spitting,
the bump and smack of tow motors roaring
into tracks or sliding and clicking in on electricity.
Walking through the endless warehouse,
I can hear the day's echoes and thoughts float
down and collect in trash. I can hear you
slicing the watermelon with a knife that shines
like treachery and deceit or like peacemaking.

Months before this, you told a black manager,
I hate niggers. You hate with sincerity.
A B.A. should put you in the white shirt
the black manager has. You worked hard
for your B.A. in evenings. Nigger has
nothing to do with race, you say. Nigger is
as nigger does. Nigger is a mark of the way
one goes through the world, as if we are ships.
Nigger is some bandit manner of sailing,
stinking into harbor. Nigger is not really
a person's color. A nigger cannot be a person.
One day you saw me driving on the beltway
and roared close, passing me in your Corvette,
mouth open, laughing at me, ignoring me.
Nigger is as nigger does. Run, nigger. Run.

You slice a whole watermelon because there is
all of me to feed such an indigenous food.
Smiling, you ask me to come over and take
a break with you. *Father God, bless our food.*

We sit in two chairs near the first truck door,
the one near the walkway coming into work.
I look out over the large truckyard of dirt
and trash I have to sweep. *Lord, we thank
thee.* I look into the blood flesh of fruit
that I had so much of on my grandfather's farm
as a child, and enjoyed so much with people
who loved me. I look on the blood flesh of fruit
that a doctor friend says heals the heart.
*Father God, these blessings we are about
to receive for the nourishment of our bodies.*

You spit seeds into the yard, under the moon's
white shining on the church's cross, and I eat
just enough to have broken bread. In your heart
you smash a black face with big white lips
slurping across a thick slice of watermelon.
The face turns to run and you kick it in the ass
until it falls on itself and turns back to grin again.
I get up to take my nightly nap away from all
of what it takes to be responsible for myself,
the lifting, the sweeping, the scrubbing dirt.
You get up and wipe your hands on your pants,
son of an eccentric father who died in a closet.
In the warehouse's shallow echo, you hate me.
My smile is a knife. I cut you in your dreams.

Mojo Mamba

My johnson got a reputation.
In the neighborhood they gave it
   a name—Mojo Mamba.
Met a girl one time, a fine young thing
when I was twelve, counting to thirteen.
She had breath like a chocolate milkshake,
titties on the emerge, hips like a roller rink.
My voice was gettin deep so I whispered
"What's your name, Baybay?" She said
"I'm Beverly." Down in the crown of BrownTown
at Hallelujah & Vine, O Holy Valley of Brown,
her legs smellin like aloe vera, my johnson spoke,
standing on its two round hind legs, spoke to spoke
rim to rim / sin to sin / rocking it in,

      "I'm Mojo Mamba."
      "I'm the Regulator."
      "I'm the Stimulator."
      "I'm the Ambulator."

I said "Walk on Baby," and Beverley hollered "Ow!"
I said "Walk on Baby," and she hollered twenty-four times,
and the juju juice rolled, the juju juice rolled.

What you think I grew up to be,
when my johnson was the Loch Ness Monster Be?
Said I integrated a beach in nineteen sixty-eight,
before The Souls of Black Folks shook the gate,
was cruisin the deep with octopuses and manatees,
taking a break from swimming the seas,
and my johnson rose up out of the water, sang
to the lifeguard, "I'm a one-eyed Mamma Jamma!"

The lifeguard told the white girls to make for land
and 999 Hips & Lips started turnin in the sand,
heard Mojo Mamba sing, spines tinglin
to see my Jammin Johnson sleeping in the seas.

I say I rock the world and turn it loose,
I say I rock the world and turn it loose.

Was workin in the steel mills in seventy-four,
put in four doubles and slept no more,
cause my desire was bustin steel, and when I tried
to sleep, I dreamed I was drillin trees.
Four days without the holy valley,
four days without the holy valley,
and I was a predator, a meditator, a calculator.
I went to the bar to see Sweet Sweet Shakeeta,
blue/black with leopard eyes, Sweet Shakeeta,
Black, O Dark, Blessed Black, Blue Black.
Kiss me, O Love, O Sable Sugar. Shakeeta
whisperin in the lace of lovemakinglove—
"I see. I see. Something's gone to splittin me."
I hadn't even touched Sweet Shakeeta
when she felt the vibration of Mojo Mamba,
a snake that swells to compel and dwell
forever in the dream of satisfaction.

Come, and remember in the morning.
Come, and remember in the evening.
Come, and remember in the intoxication.
Come, and declare heaven on earth.

Three weeks of solid slappin on the skin
lovin in bones slippin bones . . . Shakeeta whispered
sexy as OOOH WEEE pull on the string of love,
"Give me a cigarette."

I ain't no dream. I ain't no lie.
I ain't no words painted in the sky.
I am a real walkin round breathin
natural African man. I am a boom
boom chocolate galactic ride to ecstasy.
So says my johnson, Mojo Mamba,
and my love *ain't* no poision.
Come on, Girl, and get this love.
It won't leave you alone.

Hold it in your hand . . .
Wrap it with your tongue . . .
Open the gate to the land and lay it in . . .
Let me thunder you slow . . .
Let me thunder you slow . . .

It's the end of the world.
God asks for the key to open Jerusalem
& see me. "Where's my Originator?"
He says. "Where's my Regulator of Love?"

And I just riiiiiiiissse . . .
And I just riiiiiiiissse . . .
And I just riiiiiiiissse . . .

To all the real angels I say . . .
It's Judgment Day, don't you wanna lay . . .
It's Judgment Day, don't you wanna lay . . .
It's Judgment Day, don't you wanna lay . . .

With me?
With me?
With me?

Piggly Wiggly

for Gustavo A. Paredes

John smacks the asphalt to tectonic plates
when he strides to the sto,
creatin black continents with yellow lines,
twirlin that hammer like a baton,
whistlin in notes that make bricks blush,
and I skip behind him, naming new worlds.

We go down the aisle of cereals,
John talking in thunder about how he
starts a day, and the women
watch the black iron of the hammer,
the way it calls them into its darkness.
Cheerios, John?   Naw——————))))!
Wheaties, John?   Naw——————))))!
Raisin Bran, John?   Naw——————))))!

Goddam it, John! What we gonna eat for breakfast?
    ...lil brutha, let the mornin decide...

The whole store is filled with the way
        We Be
Unaccounted for, we invade the night memories
of lonely cashier / widows, the inseparable
closed minds doing crochet in the evening opera
of shadows on porches.
John talks in his thunder about his grandma
givin him the sermon on his hammer /
        Now Baby, don't swing it too hard.
        You might break somethin sweet!

So we gets down to the meat:

chicken wings	49 cents a lb
chicken legs	49 cents a lb
chicken feet	59 cents a lb
pig feet	69 cents a lb

John & I whisper together:

Ain't nothin like a trotter,
Nothin like sweet fat on a cleft hoof.

We grab two dozen pig feet, treasure trotters.
In the checkout line, sweat rises
from eyes gone to singing "Stand by Me"
as they gaze on John's hammer, its hard irony,
black but comely in Solomon's words.
They study the autograph on the handle
from when John drove it through the mountain
and the widow at the next cash register says
                "I been a mountain these last few years."
In a thunder clap John's voice rolls
                "You need a tunnel with a sprinkler system,
                and I can do that, too."

Outside the sun done set and rose four times.
It's alright. We stop time that way.

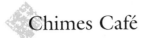
Chimes Café

for Roger Allen Jones
New American Poet

They are watching a movie out back,
and the sight of them is like a Fassbinder film
or Renoir's *Golden Coach*. I can't decide.
I have to pee. Such are God's directives.
This is the second night I have stumbled
into this ravine peopled with the conscience
of the young, of those not far from wanting.

Roger orders the air with Jackie, flirting
with her in his thick wolfhound growl.
He makes her laugh, her strands
of braids, her modern hair, dance
across the table. He tells her she
need not sleep alone, and she says she
does not. There are the children.
As Sarah said to Abraham, there are
the children, Abraham wondering why
this long career of making love, wishing.

This is the inconsequential meeting place,
where chance is the offering on a rabbit's altar.
We settle in from an alchemy's dust,
our mode of travelling, to sip the coffee,
the coffee that is real, and coffee that is fake.
That which is fake melts into the chocolate
of Jackie baring her legs from her skirt,
touching her knee, looking for that itch.

And in comes Peter laughing to see
we are here again, gaping with his German
at Roger showing me Jedi tricks, his magic

119

making people do his spirit bidding, all
sealed by Freckles' dance as she serves us
cream in the coffee   sugar in the cream.
It is time. All things collide. Roger hacks.
Jackie bows out, still not knowing why
I grunt so much instead of speaking.

In neighborhood trash, I have buried
the witch's foot, haunted pentagram,
thirteen wheels of chaos. The golden
coach is weighed with the cargo,
a commedia dell arte troupe led by
a woman addicted to adoration and
men who know only the gesture,
not the speech of perfume and hands.

Walnut Cinema

for Roger Allen Jones
New American Poet

This movie is about things we know,
about apartments with books and beer.
On the bus, I am amazed to see
another poet of Philadelphia. I am
a foreigner in the Quaker heart.
You sit in mischief like a bandit
in a British forest, your face its own disguise.
Sometimes I want to rattle your wisdom,
but I study the facades of the Main Line.

Life gave so much of itself to you
that you must take Russian vodka
on a regular basis to keep from
laughing in your waking dreams.
In the sound of paper under your foot,
in the rain and gray failure of light,
in welfare queens' lobster-dinner pleas,
in the spaces between Frank Sinatra's words,
you hear the falcon's cry that says
why we are born, why we die.

This movie is about our addictions,
hardness of life. I am sick for love.

Sam's

Teacher, why the silence?
for Major Jackson

I buy my root beer with two hands
full of nickels and dimes. Walking over
in my sweatpants, the coins felt like a pimple
big as a grapefruit, full of silver juice.
There are stars out tonight. The moon
is shaving the man's face. He is looking up
at the first floor/men's wear of the universe.
Sam's is in the basement of the universe, so
Sam's dog is dying slowly, and there are
many murders on the weekend. The fog
is waiting for the messiah to arrive
like spring, quite suddenly and above
the need left by the slush of winter.
Oh, it is winter in our hearts after all.

I put all my nickels and dimes
on the counter, a thousand little clangs
and bangs. The clerk looks at me.
I look at the clerk. It might be
more beautiful if my coins were beads
and I wore them in necklaces. Money
would grow in virtue. Buying a house
would mean spending months hauling beads
to the bank. Friends and relatives
would walk in long trains bearing beads.
There would be festivals for bead trains.
The city would stop. Beads would be served.

The clerk counts coins till he's bored.
He scoops them in his hand, smiles.
It is time to go. Maybe I gave

too much money, but I don't want
to count. It is enough work to see.
I walk home, and I see all the faces,
faces of lit rooms   faces of the trees,
faces of the street   faces of the dogs.

Sango's Marriage Song

to Osun

Dawn

I calculate a blue
over this red trail in
the ocean's song to us,
in the silver rising
past the trade. I move
block by block in
this cunning, this way
The Beast makes
an arrangement of music
broken into uncounted
patterns of wailing.
Into the end of avenues,
I look to see what birth
will roll in what I leave,
what peculiar weave
I can give to lives
still left to choose a path.
My hands move in
the unseen world,
casting heaven a mystery
to the Spirit. I hunger.
I am the thin energy
in marrow and bone.

Day

We marry
each time I knock
on the door to
the house where you

name all life.
Women fall down
to you to be given
courage and beauty.
I take this heaven
quarter with you
where we make
all men and women
in their desire.

Come whisper with me
the song we love
to spread, the blanket
of our hearts' tragedies,
of silent fires in worlds
away from this life.
Come whisper with me
as our tongues turn
to snakes rising,
naming the one wish
for eternity. I am the red
heaven opening to
your splendor, *O Beauty*,
beauty I would die for,
sweet sleeping away
as your eyes hypnotize,
hair in forgotten hymns,
toes painted red,
red, red, my heart.

Night

What child
is this, our child,
wearing its body
here on a Thursday,

the child in a pair, twins
riding my horses,
your birds in their hair?
Now gone, we know
our children are
the multitude of some
earth, some market.
Cowrie shells in the air
above us, name my love
for you, all wishes.
My tears are infinite
space in screams.
I hide them
from you. See this,
me seeing you free
to light the fires
in our blessings,
where I will always
live inside you.

I Am Born

Night calls to a forty-nine
Chevy, over the running dream
of fried porgies & collards,
notes falling to "I wonder,"
time spinning on one
hand, legs inside out in
Kongo memories. Night
song—*I am born*—
in brown, thighs I chose
over the forgotten sleep
of waiting over head cheese
& biscuits, buttermilk
gone to waste
—*I am born*—
cats in night prowls,
crows in a dance in
guns shot, hallelujah
to magic in the city.
They count the jewels
in my new breath,
twelve gem cowries,
the infinite words,
I dare not name myself
King, I dare not name
myself King. I do dare.
On the corners where
bodies beat lost lives,
there I see my landing,
I lift the Asante,
I lift the Benin,
I lift the Wolof,
I lift the Bambara,

I lift my own to Ifa,
will of heaven/home.
Conga, Boogaloo |=|
Conga, Boogaloo |=|
in this tongue
all truths of darkness.
I am born
in a bed
of blood.

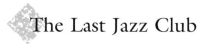

The Last Jazz Club

for Danielle Legros Georges

In a sprite room with flight
    in the ceiling,
the zippered white Bible with illustrations.
The correct way to walk is to pass time (2/4)
with some sort of affectation, being cool,
infused with the mary jane wrappers.
                       In barber shops wrapped in doo rags,
the shawls of mercy.
I am in the last measure and can't reach the chord.
Left hand, please obey the sermons . . .
        Black Harry
Measure to measure, vinegar over pig entrails,
ascension and transcendence in pots over centuries.
               Rush
into the willing loss of memory, paint peeling down to
los cucharachas.

              Where are the saints?
"This is not the most appealing source of gift-giving,"
they say after the fact of emptiness, lacing their Stacy Adams.
"How come y'all ain't got no sense of demarcation,"
they ask from the hollow of the unwritten score,
as if Lester knew this would happen.

They rush over to a TuPac grave that is unmarked,
count the gray in their hair, lift a leg with a hand
              to do the hip's hop.
Lost in the cemetery, the graves rise into the combos
of hundreds of Billie Holidays backed by a nameless ache,
silence rising like lilies of night mist.
          It is a congregation of damned discord,

disagreements fly into the mouth of a white robe over Peter,
denying the discord.

   Remove the discord and it shall be born

Be an a cappella saxophone, a horn without a horn,
da
  ba
    dada
      dede
       BOO!

Was it Hopalong Cassidy, or was it Roy Rogers?
In the kitchen with mama stealing my cornflakes...

Notes from a summer clarinet, a deflated football,
the outside trees at Christmas before drive-ins drove by,
believing the celluloid, while the celluloid believes.
Ahem, ahem,
   Borders will be established along the terrain
   of cities to be discussed in the margin notes
   written in the after train of blue coffee mugs
   above national discrepancies, no more
   territories in heaven, no Harlem, no South
   Central, no South Side, no Baltimore, no D.C.,
   the Dutiful Colored.   Borders will
   be established. Be established, damn it!
      Ahem, ahem.

Washing cars in the suds in the sun,
feeling the flesh of metal softening to kisses,
scrubbing the tires white over the black,
lifting an eye to the text in the sun, the text!

     Douglass on the sorrow songs,
     Du Bois on his two minds,
     Garvey on the ships,

Nkrumah on our mind,
Rochester on diplomacy...

Be an a cappella trumpet,
tap out courage in segregation,
dignity in the bull's rush.

The army jeeps in my breakfast, green everywhere
on my scrapple and eggs, the big dogs, the wolfbears
in deep bass barking under Grandma's knitting by the window.
This is more than *Bonanza* on Sunday nights with Lil Joe
& Hoss. I sang to old jazz albums I didn't understand
because the people who gave them to us were rich white folk
who don't know why bebop went cool or why cool went.

Will I ever understand?

Why do narcissists posit themselves as positive?
the conscious ones

I am impervious to clarity. It hurts.
Listen now to Kirkatron.

The '64 chevy supersport is the best supersport.
Pump it up on air shocks, bounce it on down, down.
Candy-apple red is my favorite color, rebellion in tint.

In the Cordon Bleu, "Crackers, anyone?"

There are black crackers, full of holes
in the soles of ghosts running in swamps,
on their naked dogs from the dogs.

Do you understand amour, its paucity?

Where is my bullets? I'm gonna shoot some spooks

in white sheets singing hymns to them selves, evil of evil
preaching.   The verse, son, the verse!

Thou shalt love thy god . . .

Miracle workers, name thy gods,
please?

me   do   re
me   me   me
me   me   me

we/me/we
night unto night
!

Composition for White Critics Who Think African-American Poets Cannot Work in Contexts of Pure Concerns for Language and Post-PostModern Twentyfirst Century Inventiveness in Lyric Expression Due to Their Self-Limiting Concerns With Language as a Means of Self-Expression and Racial/Cultural Identity in Poetry That Is Ultimately Perhaps Beautiful However Too Trite and Too Folksy to Be Post [||] Theorist Efficacy

for Jorie Graham

In lap tops on commuter flights, prop jets and peanuts
                with soda,
considering the last fate of this turning in the gyre, turning, turning
down the withering task of tunnels of white rabbits with watches
like flavo-flav, get out of here flavo-flav blues ripping over the precipice
of an amanuensis turning into an insect crab creeping into the crescendo
of hollering arias in Verdi's *Porgy & Bess*,
             I see you now.
It is time for coffee.
                Give me the complexity of knowing,
the gratitude of waking and wondering which window to thank for
   apples
in the window, becoming more red, redder than candy-apple red,
a cosmic significance of not ever having a childhood and realizing
   how such
burdens as being less than an adult require the synthesis of forms,
of flow charts   of Lotus spreadsheets,
a sexual arrangement in Tibet.   I greet you now,

after this long trek to this point, this grove of pointed hedges where
   all time
changes and you gain or you lose or you understand there is no death,
only a perception of what it means to not breathe, this timeliness
of looking back some four hundred years and figuring the power of
   being able
                           to tell some gross lie and call it history,
hoping the profit will land you a patio overlooking some wave
   crashing in
on a commercial for the Caribbean.
                Metal lands in the crevice of cradles.
What matters is this waving, weaving of textures of night sky floating
   over
the stars, as in a night before a day of raining when you can look out
   and see
the gloom to fall on all you had hoped to do, accomplishing little,
   as who
will ever know we were here if everyone falls asleep at the machine,
just before the self-conscious narrative awakens and slaps your grandma
into some bootleg distillery during the casting/cattle and you awaken
understanding nothing except thighs on the throne in the basement,
the admonition fathers give you of being kind to the dumb poor,
as the poor are all dumb—

                Listen, it's Falstaff running
in the accounting. What now, Caliban, in your old Chevrolet Impala,
   leaping
over the Wall Street disclosures and closures over any hope you ever had
of ascending to the lyceum of Tootsie Rolls, washing the hands of
   your dreams
in bleach and dishwashing liquid, oh what could be more tragic than
   dirty

beans and rice, the melting of the sauce turning to some letting out
   of blood,
away from the necessary folk richness of fables, Pitchy Patch Man

running alongside Cuchulain,
Kingston in the lurches, busy Mennonite women making shoofly pie
in the afternoon windows, in black arrangements, some Haitian cherub
peeping in through the gesticulating head of graffiti on the walls,
cross, crisscross, cross Bronx expressway, the way you wear
your clothes backwards, dirt in the bloody beans and rice,
& from the Isles,

                    screech Charlie Parker, screech,
screech and in the cruelest month take tea with the man in green
    makeup,
leaning over the bank ledge to creditors and robbers.

                In a negro bar, the negro says
"Aren't we all Sicilians here?" & we must get home by seven
as Elaine and Bobbie must get to their archery lessons, and the dogs
must get their shots, and the utility vehicle needs another manicure,
in the shadows of the lilacs in the last door—ohdear, did we
            thaw the roast—
on the train up the Mississippi to some distant point, a fading spot
in the darkening window where we will be held forever and forever,
tasting the harvest of tea leaves handed to us one day at a time,
with slices of banana bread, reading Trollope, oh god, the torture
of details in British.

                  "I want to know,"
said some minister arraigned before God on a Tuesday when
every available angelic public defender was out somewhere being
laid, out in the sun, so close and not melting, as we watch the butter
churn in the bowl and melt for homemade pound cake, having heard
the announcement about the end of downtowns, now centers
with no cartography, and we add raisins, peeping into the bowl,
ready to put it in the Mixmaster to swirl along with the flour.
           "I can't imagine a world without me,"
said the reader in the reading room, safely ensconced in words
that are capable at any time of absolute and murderous rebellion,
leaping off the shelves, abandoning syntax and punctuation,
leaving off sound to become "Now, Tommy, stop stabbing the dog"
bigger than "V" destroyed the planet we wasted before they threw

us here to Earth the virtual entertainment, chewing Big Red.
Anyone for Big Red?
The first four notes
of Dizzy's Blues, please,
in the software,

message returned to archives
your mailbox is empty

The first four notes
of Dizzy's Blues, please,
random play this time
this
time

One

Two

Three

Four

4/4 time   wide angle
sweet   fire   bird   suite

America oh my poetry America
Fade to palm trees in Los Angeles

That's the Wrap, Boys. Let's call it a movie.

THE AUTHOR

Jeff Hurwitz

Afaa Michael Weaver (b. Michael S. Weaver) is a veteran of fifteen years as a blue-collar factory worker in his native Baltimore. In 1986, he completed his B.A. at Regents College and, in 1987, his M.F.A. at Brown University. His first book of poetry, *Water Song*, appeared in 1985, and was followed by *My Father's Geography* (1992), *Stations in a Dream* (1993), *Timber and Prayer* (1995), and *Talisman* (1998). He is the recipient of a National Endowment for the Arts grant and, most recently, a fellowship from the Pew Charitable Trusts. Mr. Weaver is the editor of *Obsidian III* and the holder of an endowed chair at Simmons College in Boston, where he is the Alumnae Professor of English.